Economic Policy and the Adjustment Problem

The cartoon on the front cover, reproduced from *Punch*, London, 24 March 1926, depicts Stanley Baldwin, then Prime Minister of the United Kingdom, and his Cabinet colleagues grappling with 'the coal problem' by trying to find a way of playing down or concealing the extent of subsidies to the industry. In this Thames Essay the authors argue that the 'problem of adjustment' today is a legacy of accumulated government policies designed to assist discreetly various producer groups.

Thames Essay No. 45

Economic Policy and the Adjustment Problem

BY

Gary Banks

AND

Jan Tumlir

Gower

for the

TRADE POLICY RESEARCH CENTRE

London

First published 1986 by

Gower Publishing Company Limited
Gower House, Croft Road
Aldershot, Hampshire GU11 3HR
United Kingdom

Gower Publishing Company
Old Post Road
Brookfield, Vermont 05036
United States of America

Gower Publishing Australia
85 Whiting Street
Artamon, New South Wales 2064
Australia

British Library Cataloguing in Publication Data
Banks, Gary
  Economic policy and the adjustment problem.
  (Thames essay, no. 45)
  Bibliography: p. 92
  1. Balance of payments — Political aspects
I. Title II. Tumlir, Jan
382.1'7 HG3882
ISBN 0-566-05332-2

Library of Congress Cataloging-in-Publication Data
Banks, Gary
  Economic policy and the adjustment problem.
  (Thames essay; no. 45)
  Bibliography: p. 92
  1. Trade adjustment assistance. 2. Economic policy.
3. Free trade and protection — protection. I. Tumlir,
Jan. II. Title. III. Series.
HF1421.B36 1986   338.9   86-14934
ISBN 0-566-05332-2

ISSN 0306-6991
ISBN 0 566 05332 2

Printed in the United Kingdom by
Biddles Ltd, Guildford, Surrey

Contents

Biographical Notes

GARY BANKS has been an Assistant Commissioner at the Industries Assistance Commission (IAC) in Canberra, Australia, since late 1985, having some years earlier served as a Principal Research Economist at the Commission (1972-76). (The IAC's functions are to advise the Government of Australia on, and facilitate public scrutiny of, assistance to industry and its effects on the Australian economy.)

For most of the time between leaving and returning to the IAC, Mr Banks was an economist with the Secretariat of the General Agreement on Tariffs and Trade (GATT), in the Economic Research and Analysis Division (1976-84). Between then and his present appointment, he was a Senior Economist in the Office of National Assessments, Government of Australia.

Mr Banks graduated from Monash University, Melbourne, in 1972 and from the Australian National University, Canberra, in 1974. In 1975, he was a Lecturer in Economics in the Faculty of Military Studies, University of New South Wales. He has contributed articles on aspects of international trade and industrial policy to *The World Economy*, *Kyklos* and *Intereconomics*.

JAN TUMLIR was Director of Economic Research and Analysis at the Secretariat of the General Agreement on Tariffs and Trade (GATT) in Geneva from 1967 until early 1985. In June 1985 he was about to return to a senior teaching appointment at the University of California at Los Angeles, where he was a Visiting Professor in 1983-84, when he died suddenly at the age of 58 years. Tumlir had been a Professor of Economics at the Institut Universitaire de Hautes Etudes Internationales, University of Geneva, a member of the Council of the Trade Policy Research Centre, London, and a member of the European board of economists on *Time* magazine.

Tumlir joined the GATT Secretariat in 1964 to work in the Trade and Development Division, having previously taught economics at Yale University, New Haven, in the United States of America, where he obtained his doctorate. He studied law at Charles University, Prague, leaving Czechoslovakia in 1949 to work in the Federal Republic of Germany as a journalist before eventually going to the United States.

Besides many articles and contributions to volumes of essays, Tumlir was the author of *Protectionism: Trade Policy and Democratic Societies* (1985) and co-author of *Trade Liberalization, Protectionism and Interdependence* (1977), *Adjustment, Trade and Growth in Developed and Developing Countries* (1978) and *Trade Relations under Flexible Exchange Rates* (1980).

Preface

THE PURPOSE of this Thames Essay is to clarify thinking on the adjustment process of the market and the role of economic policy. Governments have been making heavy weather of the 'adjustment problem'. They usually see it in terms of the inherent economic difficulties posed by changes in international trade, necessitating special forms of government intervention. It is shown here though that the adjustment difficulties of contemporary economies are largely a consequence of economic policy decisions of the past. The authors argue that the real adjustment problem is a political one, calling for a restructuring of the policy-making process, which they discuss in their concluding chapter.

Gary Banks and Jan Tumlir began work on the careful presentation of the ideas in this essay when both were on the staff of the Secretariat, in Geneva, of the General Agreement on Tariffs and Trade (GATT), but much of it was written when the latter was on sabbatical leave at the University of California at Los Angeles in 1983-84 and when, soon after, the former returned to Australia. The essay was nearly finished when Tumlir, having retired early from the GATT Secretariat to return to the United States to teach and write, died suddenly at his home in Versoix on 22 June 1985. Mr Banks put the finishing touches to the essay before he joined the Industries Assistance Commission in Canberra later in the year.

Tumlir was only 58 years old when he died. Although a prolific writer, whose articles, lectures and papers for conferences had made him an influential figure in policy debates on the state of the international system of trade and payments, Tumlir had hardly begun to write what he had to offer. Some inkling of what was in store can be got from this essay.

The authors acknowledge that successive drafts of, and exerpts from, the essay have benefited from discussions with a wide range of people, including academics and officials in governments and international organizations. Among the latter, Richard Blackhurst, of the GATT Secretariat, deserves special mention.

It has to be stressed, however, that the views expressed in the essay are the personal responsibility of the authors; and they do not necessarily represent the views of members of the Council or those of the staff and associates of the Trade Policy Research Centre which, having general terms of reference, does not represent a consensus of opinion on any particular issue. The purpose of the Centre is to promote independent analysis and public discussion of international economic policy issues.

HUGH CORBET
Director
Trade Policy Research Centre

London
February 1986

Chapter 1

The 'Adjustment Problem' in Public Discussion

'Aging economies have no choice but to carry on, without contemplation of any terminal stage'

— Charles P. Kindleberger, 'The Aging Economy', *Weltwirtschaftliches Archiv*, Kiel (1978)

FOR A decade and a half, the governments of industrial countries have been grappling with a new policy problem, the 'problem of adjustment'. In public discussion, the problem has generally been identified with import competition, especially that from developing countries. Much has been written on the subject, numerous conferences have been held, many committees have been established and diverse policy measures have been implemented to deal with the problem, but no government could be said to have found a solution. On the contrary, the present crisis in international trade relations suggests that things have been getting worse.

That the focus of economic policy has been on adjustment to imports would seem at first sight to be misplaced. Imports represent only a small part of the general change that must be allowed to proceed if an economy is to grow.[1] In the normal course of economic development, import flows change slowly enough for adjustment to take place; not always smoothly perhaps, but seldom in the form of 'crises'. To appreciate why adjustment to imports has nevertheless become a major preoccupation of policy-makers, it is necessary to begin by considering the nature of the adjustment process itself.

Much of the discussion about government's role in 'structural' adjustment or the 'restructuring' of industry has fostered a misleading view of the adjustment process and structural change, as if they were able to be purposefully managed.[2] The reality is that structural adjustment is a diffuse process that begins within individual enterprises. Whole industries or sectors do not 'adjust'. It is the normal business of managers to devise strategies for dealing with changes in the market place; in fact, it is what they are paid to do. Sometimes this will involve new investment, sometimes disinvestment — the abandonment of once profitable activities — and sometimes a mixture of the two. It is the sum total of these numerous individual reactions that is perceived *ex post* as changes in the statistical aggregates used to measure structural change.

Seen in this way, structural change proceeds continuously, in response to other changes which can be most conveniently classified under the headings of supply and demand. Those on the supply side include technological innovation, both at home and abroad, and the emergence of new suppliers to the world market, together with the consequent changes in trade patterns.

Changes in the pattern of demand may either occur spontaneously (for example, as a result of changes in income which affect the demand for products in different ways) or in response to relative price changes. These antecedent changes *cause* structural change; alternatively, it may be said that structural change represents an adjustment to them. As a term of economic analysis, therefore, the word *adjustment* has a very broad meaning. It could stand, as a generic term, for all the particular changes and processes, the totality of which constitutes economic growth.

Then what is the problem? In most cases, firms should have been capable of adjusting to change, whether originating in trade or in the domestic economy — and economies should have been capable of absorbing their adjustments — without the need for government intervention. Nevertheless, in the

'crisis' industries (including agriculture), the main difficulty
has arisen precisely from the failure of the normal, cumulative
process of individual adjustments to take place. How did this
come about? No individual firm or group of firms has the
power to resist change. Failure to adjust, or responding in
the wrong way, would normally result in the eventual takeover
or liquidation of the enterprises concerned. But this, too, is
merely another form of adjustment. It is obvious that a backlog
of adjustment could not have occurred without government
assistance.

The truth is that most governments have only been paying
lip-service to the need to maintain adaptable economies. In
practice, they have acted as if adjustment were a burden,
something to be deferred until better economic (and, it is
assumed, political) times. Internationally, tensions have
increased and time for reform has been wasted by the three
major trading powers — the United States, Japan and the
European Community — accusing each other, and the
developing countries accusing all three, of trying to shift the
'burden of adjustment' on to others. It is sad to contemplate
the period since the early 1970s and to recognize that the
burden of adjustment which nobody wanted to bear *was* the
economic growth that everybody wanted.

ALTERNATIVES TO ADJUSTMENT

The overriding objective of government policy in economic
affairs is to maintain stable progress over the long run. Another
way of expressing this, and one more closely connected with
the current discussion of trade policy, is to say that the
overriding objective of all governments should be to maintain
and improve the economic order.

The very notion of order — a stable framework of
cooperation among free men and sovereign nations — is
predicated on unobstructed adjustment to changing economic
circumstances. Individuals and societies seek to improve their
position by reacting — more or less alertly, more or less
creatively — to their perceived opportunities. From this effort,

novelty is continuously generated. The laws which protect individual freedom and national sovereignty ensure that this continuous and ubiquitous effort combines to produce a massive global flow of innovation in economic activity which no government or group of governments can control.

If the global flow of change cannot be arrested, societies must adapt to it; there is no other way to maintain order. What can a refusal to adapt mean? Two different cases should be distinguished. Imagine a world in which only one country — a Himalayan kingdom or a small and quaint Old World country — refuses to accept the economic and social change proceeding abroad.

First, either its citizens must be unanimous in refusing the change, or the refusal must be enforced on an unwilling minority.

Second, the refusal implies a growing discrepancy between the country's actual and potential income as more efficient methods of production are foregone and an increasing part of the country's foreign trade is subjected to controls.

This is bound to increase the proportion of population which resents the growing social cost and is prepared to adjust to change. Thus persistence in the refusal to adjust necessitates an increase in coercion. And it is not difficult to imagine a degree of pressure or tension which the social fabric can eventually no longer bear.

This was the relatively favourable case. Imagine, instead, that a number of large industrial countries find it difficult, for political reasons, to adjust to economic change generated abroad. Since in each, the attained level of prosperity and, to an even greater extent, future growth depend significantly on foreign trade, there would immediately arise two kinds of friction or tension, internal and external, each exacerbating the other.

Internally, there would be distributional problems as economic growth at the rate to which these societies have grown accustomed slowed down. (It would have to be decided politically, in other words, who could benefit from foreign trade and who could not.)

Externally, the countries might agree that somewhat more organized trade would be a good idea; frictions would be bound to arise, however, on the questions of who should do the organizing and which products would be organized.

These illustrations announce two themes which will be important in subsequent analysis. One concerns the optimal rate of adjustment; the other, the secondary effects of adjustment assistance policies.

RATE OF ADJUSTMENT

It is widely assumed in economic policy making that prolonging the process of adjustment reduces its 'cost'. This assumption is seldom examined in any detail. Logically, for example, it would lead to the economically absurd conclusion that an infinitely prolonged adjustment, that is, no adjustment at all, should be optimal and indeed costless.

One may surmise that one of the reasons for the prevalence of this assumption is the standard procedure of theoretical economic analysis itself. To understand any economic process it must first be studied in isolation. Thus an equilibrium is assumed, a particular disturbance posited and the process of adjustment to it traced, step by step. In such theoretical analysis of an isolated case, a prolonged adjustment might well appear preferable to a rapid one. But if it is to be relevant for policy purposes, economic analysis must not stop at the isolated case. In the real world, disturbances follow on each other's heels and the policy measures adopted to control the present one influence the form in which the following ones will appear.

The notion of a continuous change, of a flow of disturbances, thus shows the 'problem' of an optimal rate of adjustment to be an artificial one. Adjustment must simply match the rate of change; if it falls below it, maladjustment will begin to cumulate, whereas a rate of adjustment exceeding the rate of change is a contradiction in terms. In short, it is as illusory to think that a relatively affluent society has a choice between more efficiency and growth, on the one hand, and greater stability and comfort from dampening down change, on the other, as it was to think of choosing between more inflation and somewhat less unemployment. In both cases the choice is solely between less discomfort now and much more of it later.

As mentioned, the measures chosen to deal with a particular disturbance influence the form of future disturbances. They do so mainly by modifying economic incentives, not only of the groups at which the policy is aimed but also those of other groups which learn from the precedent established by the policy in question. Sooner or later even these secondary effects will be felt in foreign trade and other governments may be forced to react to them. To ascertain the effects of a particular policy has been, for these reasons, perhaps the most difficult task of applied economic analysis and also the least successful.

HISTORICAL PRECEDENTS

Much of the discussion about the 'adjustment problem' has assumed or implied that the adjustment pressures since the early 1970s have been of an exceptional nature. The market, according to this view, has been overloaded by these developments, unable to 'cope'.[3] But history is full of examples of the market absorbing major structural changes without government intervention. In *The Wealth of Nations*, Adam Smith gave us the following, rather picturesque, example:

'By the reduction of the army and navy at the end of the late war, more than a hundred thousand soldiers and seamen, a number equal to what is employed in the greatest manufactures, were all at once thrown out of their ordinary employment; but, though they no doubt suffered some inconvenience, they were not thereby deprived of all employment and subsistence. The greater part of the seamen, it is probable, gradually betook themselves to the merchant-service as they could find occasion, and in the meantime both they and the soldiers were absorbed in the great mass of the people, and employed in a great variety of occupations. Not only no great convulsion, but no sensible disorder arose from so great a change in the situation of more than a hundred thousand men, all accustomed to the use of arms, and many of them to rapine and plunder. The number of vagrants was scarce anywhere sensibly increased by it, even the wages of labour were not reduced by it in any occupation, so far as I have been able to learn, except in that of seamen in the merchant-service.'[4]

It is not necessary to go back this far in history to find examples of relatively rapid and smooth adjustment to major changes. Consider the adjustment facing the economy of the United States at the end of World War II. The following two passages show the concern of economic experts at the time:

'Provision will have to be made for a minimum of 5 million soldiers returning from war; and the figure is likely to be considerably larger. A fair estimate would probably be in the vicinity of 9 million. Of these the youngest age groups will be persons who never held jobs before their entry into the army. In addition, under present forecasts, perhaps 25 million workers will have been absorbed into war industry. These will have to be replaced in peacetime industry. Included in this figure will be not less than 5 million individuals not heretofore engaged in regular labor... In the aggregate, therefore, immediate post-war readjustment will have to take care of the enormous total of perhaps 34 million individuals.'[5]

The second passage follows:

'The bill of goods our people would like to buy in peace ... differs greatly in make-up from what we are producing for war. In some lines, ships and aircraft notably, production would have to be much smaller. In metal fabricating as a whole, we would need only about one-third as much as we were producing in the middle of

1944. In consumer goods like clothing, textiles, lumber, paper, printing, and miscellaneous small industries, expansions in output of one-fourth or one-third over peak war production might be needed. In construction, trade, and service industries, the expansion above wartime levels would be still larger...That involves something more than a process of factory conversion.'[6]

By the close of hostilities, the war was estimated to be consuming some 50 per cent of the gross national product (GNP) of the United States.[7] The change was sudden. Between 1945 and 1946, Federal purchases as a proportion of GNP dropped from 42 to 12 per cent; and in 1947 they were down to 8 per cent, a level maintained in subsequent years.[8] In spite of this decline in public spending, and contrary to the pessimistic forecasts of many eminent economists, the post-war growth in GNP suffered only a temporary setback. Real GNP fell by 15 per cent in 1946, stabilized in 1947 and in 1948 grew by 4 per cent. (The initial drop in GNP undoubtedly coincided with a rise in living standards, as more production became available for domestic consumption.) Given the large stock of household savings which had been accumulated during the war, coupled with the removal of price controls, inflation was relatively high throughout this period: 9 per cent in 1946, 14 per cent in 1947 and 8 per cent in 1948; in 1949, however, consumer prices fell by 1 per cent and in 1950 there was only a 1 per cent increase.

The demobilization of labour was even greater than predicted. The armed forces declined from 11 million in 1945 to 1 million in 1947. But, in spite of this large and sudden increase in the labour force, and the need for a still larger number of workers in defence industries to switch to civilian production, the level of unemployment rose from 1 million in 1945 to only 2.3 million in 1947 and 1948 (less than 5 per cent of the total labour force and roughly one quarter of what it had been in 1939). The average duration of unemployment in this period was eight weeks. In the recession of 1949-50 unemployment rose to 3 million.

Compared with this immediate post-war structural adjustment, the adjustment demands placed on contemporary economies pale to insignificance. The conditions in which this massive structural adjustment took place are worth recounting. The government's role was, if anything, a passive one. Assets were sold to private industry on attractive terms. Price controls were removed; subsidies for food production reduced. And, as already mentioned, public expenditure was cut together with the tax burden. These changes enabled the high, post-war consumer demand to be rapidly reflected in supply. Industrial production recovered from a 14 per cent drop in 1946 to grow at an annual average rate of more than 6 cent over the next four years. Real gross private investment expenditure in 1947 was more than twice, and in 1950 nearly three times, its level in 1945.

The rapid reconversion of the American economy to peacetime production points to the two necessary conditions which must be satisfied if adjustment is to proceed rapidly and relatively smoothly.

First, the macro-economic framework must be right. This condition comprises not only adequate consumption demand but also, even more importantly, sufficiently strong investment incentives. It therefore points to the crucial policy task of maintaining economic confidence.

Second, the price system must be allowed to perform its allocative functions properly. This second condition is even more fundamental, for without it, macro-economic policy cannot function effectively.

NOTES AND REFERENCES

1. Richard Blackhurst, Nicolas Marian and Jan Tumlir, *Adjustment, Trade and Growth in Developed and Developing Countries*, GATT Studies in International Trade No. 6 (Geneva: GATT Secretariat, 1978).

2. On the abuse of the word 'structural' in economic discourse, see Fritz Machlup, 'Structure and Structural Change: Weasel Words and Jargon', *Zeitschrift für Nationalökonomie*, Vienna, Vol. 18, No. 3, 1958.

3. Note that, while Alan Powell and Peter Dixon, *Structural Adaptation in an Ailing Macroeconomy* (Melbourne: Melbourne University Press, 1979), define a 'structural adjustment *problem* ... to exist when the rate at which resources are required to be transferred patently exceeds the ability to cope of those who own and/or control the resources in question' (p. 2), this is *individual* failure and is not the same as the inability of the *market* to cope (for instance, bankruptcy does not constitute market failure).

4. Adam Smith, *An Inquiry into the Nature and Causes of the Wealth of Nations* (Indianapolis: Liberty Press, 1981) p. 436.

5. Adolf A. Berle, 'Government Function in a Stabilized National Economy', *American Economic Review*, Menasha, Wisconsin, Supplement, March 1943, p. 27.

6. Mordecai Ezekiel, 'Agriculture and Industrial Problems in Conversion from War to Peace', in Seymour E. Harris (ed.), *Economic Reconstruction* (New York: McGraw-Hill, 1945) pp. 25-26.

7. William Haber, 'Manpower and Reconversion', in Harris (ed.), *op. cit.*, p. 96.

8. This and subsequent data taken from *Economic Statistics 1900-1983* (London: The Economist Publications, 1985).

Chapter 2

History of Adjustment Assistance Policy

'The bounty to the white-herring fishery is a tonnage bounty; and is proportioned to the burden of the ship, not to her diligence or success in the fishery; and it has, I am afraid, been too common for vessels to fit out for the sole purpose of catching, not the fish, but the bounty'

— Adam Smith, *The Wealth of Nations* (1776)

'ADJUSTMENT POLICY', as a major government activity, is a creation of the 1970s. Its roots can be found, however, in a number of 'adjustment assistance' schemes devised in the two preceding decades.[1] The first of these arose as part of the Treaty of Paris, establishing in 1951 the European Coal and Steel Community, to facilitate the integration of coal and steel production in what was to become the European Community. This was followed by the establishment in 1957, under the Treaty of Rome, of the European Social Fund which provided assistance to workers (re-training, income maintenance, re-settlement subsidies) for the purpose of adjustment.[2]

Then, in the 1960s, there were two major adjustment assistance programmes established to compensate domestic interests injured by import growth resulting from the Kennedy Round of multilateral trade negotiations under the auspices of the General Agreement on Tariffs and Trade (GATT), one in the United States, which has continued in one form or another to the present time, the other in Canada.[3] In the United States the Trade Adjustment Assistance (TAA) programme began under President Kennedy's Trade

Expansion Act of 1962. It provided benefits to workers consisting of a supplementary unemployment allowance, vocational training and a grant to cover household removal expenses. Assistance to firms, following the approval of an adjustment plan, consisted of loans and loan guarantees, technical assistance, consultancy grants and special taxation provisions. In Canada, the General Adjustment Assistance Programme (GAAP), which began in 1968, was modelled on the American one. It applied to firms only, workers being covered by other more general measures.

The 1960s also saw some adjustment assistance schemes which were specific to particular sectors. The United Kingdom's Cotton Industry Scheme is one example. Its main objective was to restore the industry's competitiveness through a programme of modernization. To this end, it provided capital-scrapping compensation and investment subsidies.[4] Japan also gave similar assistance to her textiles industry under the Textile Structural Adjustment Law.[5] And, in Canada, adjustment assistance was provided to firms and workers who could demonstrate injury resulting from the liberalization conducted under the Canadian-American Automotive Agreement of 1965.[6]

RISE OF ADJUSTMENT ASSISTANCE

But the main thrust of activity occurred in the early 1970s. There were two main forces responsible. On the international plane, the North-South issue began in earnest in 1970 when the idea of a 'new international economic order' (NIEO) was formally adopted by the United Nations. A central concern of the NIEO proposals was the planned displacement of labour-intensive manufacturing production in industrial countries by imports from developing countries. Adjustment policy was seized upon as a means to that end.

'Developed countries, having in mind the importance of facilitating the expansion of their imports from developing countries, will consider adopting measures and where possible evolving a programme early in the decade for assisting the adaptation and adjustment of industries and workers in situations where they are adversely affected or may be threatened to be adversely affected by increased imports of manufactures and semi-manufactures from developing countries.'[7]

This theme was echoed repeatedly in different fora of the United Nations throughout the 'Development Decade', especially in the United Nations Conference on Trade and Development (UNCTAD) and in the United Nations Industrial Development Organization (UNIDO).[8] It was also taken up by the Development Centre of the Organization for Economic Cooperation and Development (OECD) in a widely-cited collection of essays on the subject,[9] by the International Labour Organization (ILO) which, at its Tripartite World Conference in 1976 passed a Declaration of Principles and Programme of Action, by the GATT, in the work of the Committee on Trade and Development and as part of the Multi-fibre Arrangement (MFA) and by the International Chamber of Commerce.[10]

A second reason for the increased focus on the adjustment issue was the recession, which exposed the weakened state of certain industries in developed countries that were already receiving considerable support and led to new claims for assistance. The phenomenon of absolute shrinkages in particular industries was an unaccustomed one in the post-war period and was felt to be overloading the ability of the market to cope. The quadrupling of oil prices in 1974 created a major additional need for adjustment, rendering uneconomic, in a single blow, a significant proportion of each country's capital stock. The pressure on governments to 'do something' intensified.

The natural resistance of those under pressure to adjust was manifested in a more widespread protectionist sentiment than had hitherto existed. This not only alarmed the North-South interest groups and lent additional urgency to their demands for improved market access for developing countries, it also alarmed others in developed countries who had fought for liberal trade on its own merits and were anxious to avert a retrogression. Adjustment assistance became the *cause célèbre* of the liberal trade movement in the early 1970s.

The following quotes capture some of the spirit of the literature at this time:

'The first step in a logical attack on non-tariff barriers, therefore, would be the adoption of an international Adjustment Assistance Code which would [*inter alia*] commit countries to setting up domestic adjustment assistance programmes.'[11]

'Adjustment assistance programmes should include an appropriate mechanism for anticipatory resource displacement in particularly vulnerable industries ... The criteria governing eligibility for adjustment assistance should be explicit and liberal...'[12]

'It is a preferable method than protection, since it protects, or at least supplements, real incomes without embalming or protecting patterns of production.'[13]

'Any form of adjustment assistance helps the private sector to adapt to changes, whether in government policy, the pattern of demand or the advance of technology... Adjustment assistance on a multilateral basis ... offers a rational alternative to higher trade barriers or to an excessively energetic safeguards mechanism.'[14]

'Though adjustment assistance could in principle be dealt with on a national ... basis, this could with great advantage be underpinned by an OECD approach.'[15]

Throughout the 1970s, the 'adjustment problem', spawned countless international and national conferences, study groups, committees and burgeoning quantities of literature, the central theme of which was the need for governments to devise special policy measures to facilitate the adjustment process.[16] Three theoretical rationales were commonly cited to justify government intervention: *efficiency* (reducing the 'social' cost of adjustment), *equity* (compensating the 'losers') and *expediency* (countering political resistance). In most of the literature, the term 'adjustment' was normally understood to mean adjustment to imports (especially those from developing countries).

ADMINISTRATIVE EXPLOSION

As might have been expected,' governments of industrial countries proved only too willing to expand their administrations further in order to stake out a new economic responsibility for themselves.

In the *United States*, the Trade Act of 1974 revamped the existing TAA programme by making it easier for claimants to qualify for assistance: increasing the benefits available to workers and firms and extending benefits to 'trade-impacted communities' which were eligible for grants for infrastructure projects as well as financial assistance to private investors in the area.[17] A year earlier, the Comprehensive Employment and Training Act had been passed, to coordinate the different existing manpower projects and expand employment opportunities through job-creation projects and training programmes.

In *Canada*, eligibility requirements under the GAAP were made less stringent, in amendments made in 1971 and 1973, and the focus of adjustment assistance schemes was shifted from firms to whole sectors. The Textile and Clothing Board Act of 1971 established the first such sectoral adjustment scheme whereby an approved restructuring plan could be supported by government financial assistance and temporary protection.[18]

In *Australia*, the Structural Adjustment Assistance Programme (SAA) was introduced in 1974 to provide assistance to workers (income maintenance, re-location grants) and firms (closure compensation, consultancy grants, loan guarantees) adversely affected by trade liberalization and other government policies.[19] Also in 1974, the Australian Government instituted the National Employment and Training Scheme, which subsidized (re-)training, and in 1976 the Re-location Assistance Scheme was created to promote the regional mobility of labour.

In the *European Community*, the Social Fund was upgraded in 1971 in an attempt to make it a more effective instrument for dealing with the problems of labour adjustment through the increased provision of subsidies for the retraining and regional relocation of displaced workers.[20] In addition, the countries in the Community introduced separate measures to try to deal with their own particular problems.

In the United Kingdom, the Industry Acts of 1972 and 1975 increased the power of the government to assist uncompetitive sectors and regions. The Wool Textile Industry Scheme of 1973 was the first specially designed industry-wide scheme introduced under the 1972 Act. Its objective was 'to improve the industry's competitive position by providing it with assistance to (a) modernize production facilities, (b) improve industrial structure and (c) eliminate uneconomic excess capacity'.[21] In 1975, a Job Creation Programme was introduced in the United Kingdom, under which the Manpower Services Commission was to finance labour- intensive projects.

The Netherlands established a restructuring programme in 1974 which was designed to foster the 'anticipatory' adjustment of domestic industries to imports from developing countries.[22] To be eligible for assistance, firms were required to have devised a restructuring plan, entailing the abandonment of production directly competing with exports from developing countries and its replacement by some alternative activity.

In France, the Seventh Plan for the five-year period beginning in 1976 stressed the objective of 'adjustment of our industry to increasing international competition'.[23] An Inter-ministerial Structural Adjustment Committee was created in 1974 (including both the President and the Prime Minister) to coordinate public intervention in firms experiencing adjustment difficulty. In September 1978, the Special Fund for the Adaptation of Industry was created to provide subsidies and loans to new projects in structurally-depressed regions.

West Germany, Italy and Belgium, and Sweden, outside the Community, instituted broad adjustment-assistance measures and manpower programmes, although most were not related specifically to trade.[24] In *Japan*, adjustment-assistance schemes had already been devised for particular industries, such as coal and textiles, in the 1960s. In 1978, an act was passed (Special Measures for the Stabilization of Specific Depressed Industries) which formalized the procedure for government intervention in problem industries, the stated objective of which was to reduce their production capacity.[25] Some fourteen industries, including steel, shipbuilding and textiles, were selected for restructuring. In addition, a number of manpower policy measures were implemented in the 1970s, including the New Vocational Training Plan, which provided for training in basic skills at government institutions, and the Employment Stabilization Fund, to assist labour mobility.

This enthusiastic response of governments to the 'adjustment problem' received a mixed reception. At first there was a period of almost general if muted approval. This is well illustrated by the relatively conciliatory tone of a report prepared by the UNCTAD Secretariat for the annual meeting of the Trade and Development Board in mid-1977.[26] Although stressing that, in most of the countries reviewed, more could be done to facilitate adjustment to imports from developing countries, the report was confident that existing programmes could be adapted for that purpose. The Netherlands programme, with its developing-country focus, was singled out as a model for other governments.[27]

FALL FROM GRACE

The initial approval of the efforts of governments gradually gave way, however, to increasingly widespread concern about the nature of some of the intervention taking place in the name of adjustment assistance.[28] It appeared that, far from facilitating the shrinkage of uncompetitive sectors, adjustment subsidies were frequently being used to prop them up. This was especially true of the assistance schemes for what were becoming known as the 'crisis' industries: shipbuilding, steel, textiles, clothing and footwear.

Much of the assistance provided to firms in these industries was based on the premise that a programme of 'modernization' could restore their competitiveness. For example, a central element in the United Kingdom's Wool Textile Scheme of 1973 was the provision of investment subsidies to firms on condition that their old machines were physically destroyed.[29] W.M. Corden, the Australian economist, dismissed this approach as 'straightforward protection'.[30] In fact, adjustment-assistance schemes for particular sectors frequently included trade restrictions, in order to give the industry a 'breathing space' to carry out its re-structuring programme.[31] Other measures designed for the same purpose included production subsidies, tax write-offs, 'temporary' employment subsidies *et cetera*.

A number of re-structuring programmes, motivated by the perceived need to reduce the capacity of problem industries as well as to modernize them, encouraged mergers and cartel arrangements. Among the best-known examples have been the Davignon Steel Plan for the European Community — which specified production quotas for member countries and minimum prices (supported by export restraints on external suppliers to the Community) — and the sectoral re-structuring plans in Japan, especially under the Depressed Industries Act of 1978, referred to previously.[32]

Enter 'Positive' Adjustment Policy

These developments were widely criticized and, in the late 1970s, a quest for greater purity in adjustment policy began. A number of papers appeared at this time which analysed the measures in place and suggested preferred forms of adjustment assistance.[33] At the international level, the OECD organized an intensive five-year programme of work under the pleonastic banner of 'positive adjustment policy'. A *communiqué* of the OECD Council issued in June 1978 proclaimed that:

'A progressive shift to *more positive* adjustment policies must ... be an integral part of the programme of better balanced growth in the world economy.'[34]

At about the same time, however, evidence was accumulating that many measures of intervention which *were* designed to play a 'more positive' role in the adjustment process were proving either ineffective or unworkable. One example is the Trade Adjustment Assistance programme in the United States, mentioned previously, which was transformed in 1974, following widespread criticism of its operation in the preceding twelve years.[35] Provisions for adjustment assistance to workers and firms were expanded and made more generous; assistance was extended to whole communities experiencing adjustment difficulties and the criteria for granting assistance were considerably relaxed. These changes, together with greater efforts to promote the programme by its new administration, the Department of Labor, provoked a sharp rise in disbursements, which soon reached unsustainable levels. Payments to workers alone increased from $79 million in 1975-76 to about $1 billion in both 1980 and 1981.[36] Moreover, contrary to expectations, the vast expansion in spending on the TAA had no noticeable effect in improving the efficiency of the adjustment process or reducing political pressures for protection.[37] As a result, the government was obliged to undertake a new 'reform' of the TAA under the Omnibus Budget Reconciliation Act of 1981, tightening the eligibility criteria once more and reducing benefits.[38]

The selective measures of intervention, in which public assistance was provided to crisis industries for 'restructuring proposals', were frequently marked by failure. This applied not just to the modernization or 'rehabilitation' schemes, referred to above,[39] but also to the 'anticipatory' schemes designed to guide the transfer of resources to more promising alternative activities. The Dutch Government, reviewing its experience with the programme that had found such favour with UNCTAD, was forced to conclude that 'the idea that an innovative, forward-looking restructuring programme could be carried out has proved to be largely illusory'.[40]

NOTES AND REFERENCES

1. Note the much earlier example given by Charles Kindleberger: 'It is seldom mentioned that when the Corn Laws [in the United Kingdom] were repealed, a fund of £2 million was established to extend the draining techniques of high farming among the landowners in England and another fund of £1 million was established in Ireland. In France, Louis Napoleon put 40 million francs into a loan fund for adjustment assistance to producers adversely affected by the Cobden-Chevalier treaty of 1860.' Charles Kindleberger, *Government and International Trade*, Princeton Essays in International Finance No. 129 (Princeton: Princeton University, 1978) p. 4.

2. *Adjustment Assistance Measures*, TD/121 (Geneva: UNCTAD Secretariat, 1971).

3. Charles Frank, *Foreign Trade and Domestic Aid* (Washington: Brookings Institution, 1977).

4. Caroline Miles, *Lancashire Textiles: Case Study of Industrial Change* (Cambridge: Cambridge University Press, for the National Institute of Social and Economic Research, 1968).

5. Kiyoshi Kojima, 'The Japanese Experience and Attitudes towards Trade Adjustment', in Helen Hughes (ed.), *Prospects for Partnership: Industrialisation and Trade Policies in the 1970s* (Baltimore: Johns Hopkins Press, 1973) p. 256.

6. Frank, *op. cit.*

7. Paragraph 35 of the United Nations International Development Strategy, cited in the UNCTAD document, *Adjustment Assistance Measures*, *op. cit.*

8. Various UNCTAD reports and *Redeployment of Industries from Developed to Developing Countries: Studies Undertaken by UNIDO*, ID/B/222 (Vienna: United Nations Industrial Development Organization, 1979).

9. *Adjustment for Trade: Studies on Industrial Adjustment Problems and Policies* (Paris: OECD Secretariat, 1975).

10. *Adjustment Assistance Measures*, Report of the Commission on the Expansion of International Trade, 102/86 (Paris: International Chamber of Commerce, 1970). Also, in 1981, the ICC sponsored

a conference, held in the GATT building, on the topic of Structural Adjustment.

11. Gerard and Victoria Curzon, *Global Assault on Non-tariff Trade Barriers*, Thames Essay No. 3 (London: Trade Policy Research Centre, 1972) p. 32.

12. *Adjustment Assistance Measures*, *op. cit.*, pp. 9-10.

13. W.M. Corden, *Trade Policy and Economic Welfare* (Oxford: Clarendon Press, 1974) p. 111.

14. Geoffrey Denton, Seamus O'Cleireacain and Sally Ash, *Trade Effects of Public Subsidies to Private Enterprises* (London: Macmillan, for the Trade Policy Research Centre, 1975) p. 235.

15. David Lea, 'International Adjustment Assistance', in C. Fred Bergsten (ed.), *Toward a New World Trade Policy: the Maidenhead Papers* (London: Lexington, 1975) p. 313.

16. See the bibliography in Martin Wolf, *Adjustment Policies and Problems in Developed Countries*, Staff Working Paper No. 349 (Washington: World Bank, 1979).

17. *Certifying Workers for Adjustment Assistance: the First Year Under the Trade Act* (Washington: General Accounting Office, 1977).

18. Frank, *op. cit.*

19. For details of the Australian schemes, including budget allocations, see the *Annual Reports* of the Industries Assistance Commission, Canberra.

20. *Bulletin of the European Communities*, Commission of the European Community, Brussels, March 1971.

21. *The Wool Textile Industry Scheme* (London: Her Majesty's Stationery Office, for the Department of Trade and Industry, 1978) p. 3.

22. *Memorandum on the Restructuring of the Netherlands Economy and Development Cooperation* (The Hague: Ministry of Economic Affairs, 1974).

23. *Rapport sur l'adaptation du Septième Plan* (Paris: Commissariat Générale au Plan, 1978).

24. Surveys of national adjustment programmes and policies are contained in the following publications: the report of the OECD, *Adjustment for Trade: Studies on Industrial Adjustment Problems and Policies*, *op. cit.*; the report of the General Accounting Office (GAO) in the United States, *Considerations for Adjustment Assistance under the 1974 Trade Act: a Summary of Techniques used in Other Countries* (Washington: General Accounting Office, 1979); and *Employment, Trade and North-South Cooperation* (Geneva: International Labour Office, 1981).

25. *News from MITI*, Ministry of International Trade and Industry, Tokyo, 24 March, 1978.

26. *Adjustment Assistance Measures*, TD/B/C.2/171 (Geneva: UNCTAD Secretariat, 1977).

27. *Ibid*, p. 17. See also Santosh Mukherjee, *Restructuring of Industrial Economies and Trade with Developing Countries* (Geneva: International Labour Office, 1978) p. 73.

28. See A.J. Sarna, 'International Guidelines for Industrial Adjustment Policies', *Journal of World Trade Law*, Geneva, November-December 1981.

29. The report of the British Department of Trade and Industry on *The Wool Textile Industry Scheme*, *op. cit.* For an early article which shows the costliness of 'capital destruction subsidies' applied to the textile industry in the United Kingdom, see Simon Rottenburg, 'Adjustment to Senility by Induced Contraction', *Journal of Political Economy*, Chicago, December 1964.

30. Corden, *op. cit.*, p. 111.

31. The 'breathing space' approach to adjustment policy is well illustrated by the history of the Multi-fibre Arrangement. The temporary protection which it enshrined is now over twenty years old and makes a mockery of Article 1(4): 'Actions taken under this Arrangement shall not interrupt or discourage the autonomous adjustment processes of participating countries.' See *Textiles and Clothing in the World Economy* (Geneva: GATT Secretariat, 1984).

32. On Japan, see J. Mark Ramseyer, 'Letting Obsolete Firms Die: Trade Adjustment Assistance in the United States and Japan', *Harvard International Law Journal*, Cambridge, Massachusetts, Fall 1981.

33. For example, in Australia, the Industries Assistance Commission (an early advocate of adjustment assistance) noted: 'In the light of past experience with adjustment measures, the Commission considers that it may be appropriate to re-appraise the need for such measures and the form they should take. It is essential that adjustment measures include elements that actually promote adjustment and do not serve entirely as defensive measures to retard change.' *Annual Report 1979-80* (Canberra: Industries Assistance Commission, 1980) p. 38. See also Wolf, *op. cit.*, p. 27, and Ramseyer, *op. cit.*

34. 'Policies for Adjustment: some General Orientations', Council *communiqué* of 15 June 1978, reprinted in *Positive Adjustment Policies: Managing Structural Change* (Paris: OECD Secretariat, 1983) p. 111.

35. 'Bitter memories still survive from that period of illusory promises in which the hopes of workers were raised only to be dashed by repeated denials of benefits.' See Kent G. Cprek, 'Worker Adjustment Assistance: Black Comedy in the Post-Renaissance', *Law and Policy in International Business*, Washington, 1979, p. 595.

36. For details, see James A. Dorn, 'Trade Adjustment Assistance: a Case of Government Failure', *Cato Journal*, Washington, Winter 1982, p. 875.

37. *Restricting Trade Act Benefits to Import-affected Workers who cannot Find a Job can save Millions*, HRD-80-11 (Washington: General Accounting Office, 1980); *Trade Adjustment Assistance for Workers: Program Growth and Possible Changes* (Washington: Congressional Research Service, Library of Congress, 1981); 'The Upsurge in TAA', *Morgan Guaranty Survey*, New York, July 1980; and Dorn, *op. cit.*

38. The budgetary collapse of the TAA after the 1974 Trade Act was predicted in 1973 in a penetrating article by Dean Hinton, 'Comment: Policy Issues', in Hughes (ed.), *op. cit.* He noted: 'UAW is proposing a form of adjustment assistance, but when that form of adjustment assistance is put in the political context of the United States in the 1970s, the budgetary amounts implied are far, far greater than even the top estimates' (p. 179).

39. Frank, *op. cit.*; Wolf, *op. cit.*; Harold A. Bratt, 'Assisting the Recovery of Import-injured Firms', *Law and Policy in International Business*, No. 1, 1974; and Victoria Curzon Price, *Industrial Policies in the European Community* (London: Macmillan, for the Trade Policy Research Centre, 1981).

40. *Development Cooperation and the World Economy* (The Hague: Ministry of Economic Affairs, 1979) p. 82.

Chapter 3

Is There a Case for Adjustment Assistance?

THE FAILURE of adjustment-assistance programmes has tended to be blamed on the particularities of their design and implementation, the alleged shortcomings of the administrators of the programmes and inadequate funding.[1] Rarely has the intellectual case for adjustment assistance itself been questioned. This attitude is typified by one proponent's conclusion that 'even though the adjustment assistance concept is *sound in theory*, it has been a disaster in practice'.[2] Just how 'sound in theory' is adjustment assistance? The case rests on three arguments, each of which warrants a more critical examination.

'Costs' of Adjustment

'The person who loses wealth either via transfer of goods or the reduction of their exchange value is suffering a real loss of wealth, but not a cost. That loss is different in principle, in kind and in fact from a cost'

— Armen A. Alchian, 'Cost',
International Encyclopedia of Social Sciences (1968)

It is alleged that changes in comparative advantage, while on the whole beneficial, occasion 'adjustments costs', which may be reduced or eliminated by appropriate government intervention. The popular expression of this idea can be found in the notion of the 'social cost' of adjustment, which seems to suggest that adjustment is a costly activity for society as a whole.

There has been considerable confusion surrounding the whole discussion of adjustment costs, most of which can be traced to careless usage of the terms 'cost' and 'social cost', especially in non-professional parlance. In economics, *cost* can only arise from a decision; namely, a person's (or a government's) deliberate decision to sacrifice specific alternatives in the pursuit of a given course of action. The cost of the chosen activity, then, is the highest-valued alternative foregone. The *total* costs of producing something can be separated into the 'private' contractual outlays of a producer and 'external' costs, not reflected in the accounts of the producing unit, which the production activity imposes on bystanders. These 'externalities' are costs every bit as much as the monetary outlays on inputs, for they use up valued resources, even if the producer is not obliged to pay for them. (The classic example of a production externality involves a polluting factory and the implicit input 'clean air'.[3])

It was perhaps unfortunate, in view of the subsequent misunderstandings, that in 1920 Arthur C. Pigou christened the total internal and external costs arising from individual choice, the '*social* cost of producing X'.[4] Here the anthropomorphic conception of society is implicated, as if it were 'society' that was producing X. It would have helped clarity of interpretation if the expression 'social cost' had been reserved just for the external costs borne by those who did not participate in the production decision.

Nevertheless, in the context of production, these concepts of costs, irrespective of their labels, have meaning. But what could be the costs, properly defined, of *adjustment* or *change*? These have been characterized in the literature as: (i) declines in wealth that certain individuals may suffer in a changing economic environment and (ii) output foregone through transitional unemployment of displaced labour and capital.

Declines in Wealth

An example of the first usage can be found in the following passage from a recent OECD publication:

'If demand and supply factors cause an industry to decline, and in particular if it happens at an excessive rate, *this creates considerable costs*: workers may have to accept lower wage increases or may lose their jobs... In addition, capital may have to be written off before the technical end of the capital good's life span.'[5]

It suggests that adjustment costs comprise the decline in the values of private assets or of particular property rights, including the value of labour engaged in those occupations against which comparative advantage is shifting.

It is better, however, to speak of changes in *relative* asset values, to call attention to the fact that this decline in wealth is compensated by, and indeed makes possible, increases in assets and asset values elsewhere in the economy. Such declines in particular asset values in consequence of new activities developing within an economy are called '*pecuniary* externalities' and this may explain why they are sometimes confused with social costs. Indeed, the label and the whole concept are fundamentally misleading in that true external costs always involve a misallocation of resources, reducing the total wealth of the society below what it could be. Pecuniary externalities have no adverse effects on total wealth; they can be considered pure — costless — transfers. It promotes a fuller understanding to consider such changes as the vehicle of growth — the particular value losses being a necessary condition of the gains realized elsewhere. This is no less true when the activity reducing the value of particular assets in the economy is located abroad. The loss of comparative advantage in a particular line of production automatically entails a corresponding gain in others.

Thus the losses in asset values resulting from changes in comparative advantage are clearly not external costs, but they are not private costs either. They do not result from any conscious decision by the injured parties. It is the mere existence of a more efficient method, the *potential* availability of cheaper supplies, that reduces the value of these assets. Where there is no alternative foregone, the economist cannot speak of 'cost'. This also applies to the extreme cases in which the original loss in capital values stemming from changes in the external economic environment represents a net loss to the economy at large. One example is the demise of the Chilean nitrates industry, a quantitatively important resource with no alternative uses. The point is that the Chilean Government was powerless to prevent or reverse the loss to its economy.

An investment decision is about converting generalized (liquid) purchasing power irrevocably into real assets, the value of which will be determined throughout their lives by the essentially uncertain prospect of their future earnings. These assets may be valued in three different ways:

(a) by their *book values*, reflecting the (non-economic) conventions of cost accounting and tax system;

(b) by their *market values*, reflecting their discounted earnings in the market as it is actually constituted; and

(c) by their *social values*, which are determined by the rate of return that each capital good can earn when the output for which it has been shaped is obtained in the most efficient manner known.

Now it is true that, although nothing can be done about a decline in the social value of capital, governments can attempt to maintain its market value by subsidizing the return on it with an income transfer from the society at large. This policy reaction, however, *creates* social cost instead of reducing or removing it.[6] Consumers suffer and other industries suffer; and resources remain tied in low-productivity occupations, while economic development in conditions of unobstructed trade would push them towards higher productivity uses. A final irony is that only a small proportion of the owners of assets in the protected industry can be helped by policies of this kind. Those (for example, pension funds) who hold the equity of the protected industry in diversified portfolios will lose on balance, relative to the development which would have taken place if the progress of the industry had remained unobstructed. This is because the adverse effect of protection on the rest of the economy — hence on the valuation of the rest of the portfolio — must more than offset whatever favourable effect there may be on the equity of the protected firms.

Transitional Unemployment

The second alleged source of 'adjustment costs' is the transitional unemployment that is associated with the displacement and reallocation of labour and capital. The costs are commonly measured by an imputed value-in-employment for the idle factors and sometimes by the charge that the support of the unemployed implies for public budgets.[7]

If output were foregone unnecessarily during the adjustment process — that is, if something could be done about it, without losing more output in the process — then this would indeed be a social cost, although it does not necessarily follow that it would represent a cost of *adjustment*. To determine the true nature and origin of such cost, the analysis must be developed more systematically. In the *perfect competition model*, which postulates an ideal apolitical world of perfect foresight where all resource flows are frictionless and instantaneous (displaced workers immediately re-employed), it is clear that adjustment to a change in demand or supply (for example, increased imports) cannot result in any lost output and there could be no social cost.

At a lower level of abstraction, *an 'imperfect', yet efficient, economy* can be imagined in which

(a) the micro-economic role of government is confined to protecting property rights, making competition work and supplying pure public goods and

(b) economic agents make decisions in an environment where there is risk, uncertainty and positive transaction costs.

In such a world, there would be adjustment frictions: workers displaced by imports would not enter new jobs immediately; they would have to search for them, perhaps shift localities, and in the meantime they would not be 'producing' anything. But this minimum search time does not represent a cost to society because it reflects a necessity which cannot be changed by human will. In fact, the minimum search time between jobs in such an economy is itself socially valuable (and should lengthen with higher average income levels).[8] It gives individuals the opportunity to correct past errors, to find jobs that are more satisfying to them and to contribute more to GNP. (Labour will on average always be moving from lower-valued to higher-valued uses in this setting.) In any case, in the world posited here, frictions of this kind would be short in duration, relatively insignificant in extent, and social provision for reducing the hardship they cause could be easily made from the increment to national income which adjustment makes possible.[9]

Finally, we descend to our *contemporary 'mixed-up' economies*, made rigid and inefficient by an accumulation of policy measures and other organizational impediments to the proper operation of the market. (These are examined in some detail in Chapter 5.) Even in this situation, most of the capital and labour released from uncompetitive firms will eventually find new employment. Nevertheless, serious imperfections in the legal-institutional framework in which the market operates can cause the transitional unemployment of labour and capital to be both extensive and prolonged. Where these imperfections are correctible, the loss of output is in principle avoidable and thus strictly unnecessary — a social cost, strictly speaking. But that also means that it cannot be attributed to the (need for) adjustment. It may well be that the stress of change in periods of cyclical downturn calls attention to the costs of market impediments, while in the preceding period their existence was either unnoticed or considered acceptable. In that case, the correction of these costly imperfections would be an *additional benefit*, rather than a cost of adjustment.

It should be further borne in mind that these costly market impediments reduce the efficiency of adjustment to *all* changes, not merely that of adjustment to imports. In the total of social costs so occasioned, those associated with imports usually represent a small fraction; more often than not, it is the market impediments themselves which make the import-competing industry vulnerable to import competition in the first place.[10]

It emerges that what is commonly described as the cost of adjustment is caused not by the necessary adjustment as such, but by *correctible* pre-existing market imperfections. Where these imperfections cannot be corrected, or only by incurring greater cost in the process (for example, because they are institutions forming part of the constitutionally-legitimate social fabric of an economy), it is impossible to speak of social cost at all. An institutional setting that embodies the value judgments of society is a *parameter* of the market and should not be measured against an apolitical ideal, such as the perfect competition model.[11]

The Second Best
This is relevant to those attempts to justify adjustment assistance on second-best grounds. The presumption is that there are certain market distortions impeding the re-allocation of displaced factors which, for (usually unspecified) political reasons, cannot be tackled directly.[12] Instead, economists have set about devising ingenious schemes of 'countervailing' action involving lump-sum subsidies and taxes.[13] The intuitive appeal of this approach is shattered, however, by the realization that the initial, untouchable distortions are either implicitly or explicitly the *outcome* of government policies in the past. The second-best approach fails to explain how a government which at one time implemented certain measures (or allowed certain private organizational devices to develop) *and is now politically stuck with them*, could be politically capable of offsetting these measures by indirect means. Moreover, as was noted in an article in *Economic Inquiry*:

'In its broadest form the distortion-creating constraint represents an economic advantage to a particular sector of the economy. The advantage is politically conferred and the persistence of the distortion is determined by the structure of the political process (e.g., majority rule or unanimity, freedom of entry, etc.). Once the political choice has been effected within a generally accepted democratic framework, to describe it as being 'politically infeasible to remove' is to present, not a constraint on policy, but an instance of its achievement and endorsement.'[14]

In addition to these internal contradictions, the second-best approach presumes (i) that government has the *technical* ability to identify and implement second-best solutions (solutions which are especially complex in the case of adjustment assistance, requiring variable 'dynamic subsidies' and the like)[15] and (ii) that the additional interventions will themselves give rise to no social cost. The appropriateness of these presumptions is considered in subsequent chapters. It might just be noted here that, in practice, the bulk of adjustment policy measures — crisis cartels, modernization schemes, supplementary unemployment benefits *et cetera* — bear no resemblance to the ingenious solutions proposed by second-best theorists.[16]

EQUITY CONSIDERATIONS

'When considerations of national policy make it desirable to avoid higher tariffs, those injured by that competition should not be required to bear the full brunt of the impact'

— John F. Kennedy, Message to the United States Congress on the Reciprocal Trade Agreements Program (1962)

The argument for adjustment assistance on equity grounds is often associated with, but conceptually distinct from, the argument based on the presence of adjustment costs. It suggests that, since the benefits of trade are widely spread, whereas the (lesser) losses to which it may give rise are concentrated on relatively small groups, equity demands that the latter should be compensated by transferring to them a part of the benefits.[17]

It is essential to distinguish two situations in which this argument is employed. It has some validity in the context of *trade liberalization.* Here the equity issue relates to property values enhanced by the government act which instituted protection in the first place; these values could be reduced by the subsequent government decision to reduce or dismantle that protection. As the earlier discussion shows, the level of protection is an important determinant of asset values (that is, private or market, not social asset values) in the protected industry. Those individuals who obtained a capital gain when protection was instituted might have already realized it; and the subsequent owners who acquired these assets at their new prices suffer a loss when protection is reduced.[18] (The same reasoning holds, it should be added, for the specific property rights — such as seniority, pension rights and the human capital accumulated through training and experience — acquired by the workers employed in the protected industry.) As has been pointed out in an important essay, the transition from the actual state to the preferred one is not without private losses; and the normative significance of these transitional losses 'which arise because pre-existing rules and institutions have legitimized claims and expectations' has not been sufficiently emphasized.[19]

In principle, the losses imposed by policy reversals can be minimized by the change being announced sufficiently in advance. In the case of changes in trade policy, the institutional framework in which they occur ensures that these conditions are satisfied.

The negotiations for trade liberalization take a number of years and industries which will suffer major reductions in protective barriers receive an early warning.

The agreed liberalization is normally then implemented in pre-announced stages, again giving the affected industries time to adjust.

Finally, there are escape clauses in these agreements to help industries which seem to be overwhelmed by imports, in spite of the anticipatory adjustment period.

It was on the basis of this last consideration, that the escape clauses provided for in commercial treaties and national statutes traditionally stipulated that emergency protection would be available to domestic producers suffering injury through an increase in imports *in consequence* of the tariff concessions specified in the treaty. For example, the Trade Expansion Act of 1962 in the United States authorized adjustment assistance in cases where the 'major cause' of injury was an absolute increase in imports resulting 'in major part' from past trade concessions.[20] These criteria, although much criticized subsequently for being too harsh, were in fact perfectly appropriate to the declared equity objectives of the TAA programme. (The fact that actual disbursements were relatively small is irrelevant, except as an indication of the unimportance of injury through trade liberalization at that time.)

It is a very different situation when adjustment assistance is advocated as an alternative to *increased protection*. In the former case, the equity claim arises from the fact that the values of private property rights have been changed by a government action. In the situation now discussed, government is called upon to mitigate the adverse consequences of economic competition (a normal state of economic life which benefits society at large) for a particular group. Indeed, the government is held to ransom, the powerful pressure groups demanding more protection or else an acceptable alternative.

In a situation of this kind it is impossible to justify adjustment assistance on equity grounds. Equity, or justice, is nothing if not a general principle; and the feature of 'widespread benefits and concentrated costs' is present in *all* instances of economic innovation, whether originating at home or abroad. Societies do not systematically compensate for the adverse effects of innovation on individuals, for several good reasons. One is, properly, equity: individuals should be supported by society for a general reason, such as poverty. If the adverse effects of a particular event, such as innovation, were selected for compensation, many of those qualifying might not be poor at all. The main reason, however, is that the effects of such a policy are bound to be far-reaching and unforeseeable. A government's obligation to compensate all the adverse effects which economic progress has on the welfare of particular groups would amount to socializing all the major economic risks. It is impossible to form a reliable *ex ante* judgment as to all those side-effects of such a policy which can be subsumed under the label of 'moral hazard', or to estimate the policy's effects on the incentive to innovate; all that can be said is that the whole social order would be profoundly changed. (These issues are considered in the next chapter.) It should be noted, though, that the balance of interests and political forces in society is strongly tilted against such a sweeping change. In all cases of domestic innovation, there is a well-defined group of producers benefiting from it, balancing out the adversely affected group of producers who have to adjust. In that political situation, the claim for special compensation is not likely to be raised.

One may ask whether it would it be a sufficiently general principle if the government decided to compensate domestic producers for all adverse effects of changes in comparative advantage. On any theory of justice, this, too, would represent an arbitrary designation of particular change as a cause for compensation. There is no reason to suppose that international shifts in comparative advantage are more frequent, drastic or harmful to particular groups than economic change of domestic origin. In effect, changes in international comparative advantage *originate* from changes within national economies. As it would be more general, however, a policy seeking an equal treatment of export and import-competing industries would represent an improvement on a policy compensating damages caused by imports only. Unfortunately there is a prohibitive political consideration. Export industries may be as often affected by adverse shifts in comparative advantage as import-competing ones. But they could not benefit to the same extent from a re-structuring financially assisted by the government. Their sales in foreign markets would soon run up against internationally sanctioned measures prohibiting subsidies and unfair competition.

POLITICAL EXPEDIENCY

'The role of the economist in discussion of public policy seems to me to prescribe what should be done, politics aside, and not to predict what is politically feasible and then to recommend it'

— Milton Friedman, 'Comment on Monetary Policy', *Essays in Positive Economics* (1953)

As described, the equity argument for adjustment assistance has some limited justification in the context of adjustment to reductions in existing trade barriers. In situations in which the equity argument does not hold — namely when increased protection is being demanded — adjustment assistance has still been advocated on political grounds.[21] The 'expediency' argument presupposes that government cannot afford to withdraw or refuse a request for protection unless some alternative form of assistance (a bribe, in effect) is provided.[22]

This line of argument is one which commonly confronts those who propose policies on the basis of general criteria, such as economic efficiency. Unless such advice is tempered by the probability of it being accepted, the adviser is charged with being 'unrealistic' or naïve. 'That's alright in theory, but it won't work in practice' is a comment of such universal application that Immanuel Kant was provoked to write a book under that title.[23] A fundamental issue, however, is whether 'political feasibility' is ever a sufficiently determinate concept for it to provide a useful criterion for economic policy decisions. Who can know in advance whether a given line of action is politically feasible or not?

Economists tend to abandon the scientific method of their profession when it comes to politics. Their record in political second-guessing, though, is not a flattering one. Even as astute a member of the profession as Lord Keynes was open to criticism on that score. One example is his advocacy of a tariff for Britain in 1931. As has been observed: 'Keynes as professional economist thought devaluation was appropriate at that time, but Keynes as amateur political scientist thought that *politically infeasible*, so he recommended a tariff. Six months later, Britain devalued, but the tariffs introduced in that year are still in place.'[24]

The assignment of 'political feasibility quotients' requires knowledge of existing attitudes, as well as the strength with which they are held and how they will be reflected in action. It is also necessary to know how attitudes will be affected by the force of ideas and events and, in particular, by the policy proposals being contemplated and the political skill with which they are presented and defended.[25] Perhaps the most remarkable instance of the force of ideas upon attitudes is Adam Smith's *The Wealth of Nations*, a book devoted to the promotion of free trade, which was published in 1776 when its antithesis, mercantilism, was orthodoxy. It took a mere 70 years for his truly radical ideas to become the new orthodoxy (an event, moreover, which Smith himself considered not to be politically feasible[26]).

It may be worth examining the foundations of the 'realistic' argument that the refusal of protectionist demands requires bribery. Vested interests, pressure groups, are minorities by definition. Their function is to re-distribute income from society at large to their own members. If government believes this to be against the interests of society, then on ethical grounds it has no business in trying to bribe such pressure groups. Practical politics may require, however, that ethics give ground occasionally to electoral considerations. But since these pressure groups *are* minorities after all — and anti-social minorities at that — the electoral consequences of offending them should not be grave in most cases, provided that the electorate at large has a proper understanding of what is at stake.

Perhaps import-competing groups are felt to be special minorities in this respect, because they are able to appeal to the xenophobia latent in every society, whereas the conflicts engendered by other minority groups are internalized. Or perhaps society gives these groups its support because it does not understand the costs and distributional consequences which are entailed in that support. In these circumstances, however, the proper function of democratic government is not to ignore, let alone help promote, the misconceptions and ignorance on which pressure groups depend, but to bring about a proper understanding in the community at large of the consequences of different policies. (As has been argued, 'no policy which is for the advantage of the people is incapable of being effectively explained to them'.[27]) The alternative is to try to bribe (and stay friends with) producer groups, and while this is undoubtedly more congenial to politicians, it represents an escape from their main constitutional responsibility. This has far-reaching consequences which, as later chapters will attempt to show, are at the heart of the 'adjustment problem' itself.

Those proposing compensation as the 'price to pay' for liberal trade — with the implication being that it will be a *small* price relative to the benefits — must explicitly address two important questions:

(a) What sort of bribe (and how much) will be needed in each instance?

(b) What will be its 'general equilibrium' effects?

Consideration of the first question reveals that the problem with a bribe is that, unlike compensation to redress an injury, there is no theoretical basis for determining *ex ante* the sum to be provided. This will evolve through a bargaining process between the representatives of government, industry and labour. There are a number of reasons for believing that the smallest amount needed to bribe these groups successfully will normally be very large. The very fact that the government could have been put in this position at all would indicate that the industry has considerable bargaining strength. For their part, the vested interests will attempt to extract as much as they can from the government. The minimum compensation acceptable to them would be equal to the expected net returns from staying in an adequately protected industry less the expected net returns from alternative employment.

A number of studies have shown that many workers in declining industries are less adaptable and employable than the average.[28] For such people, job security (the *status quo*) understandably takes precedence over the alternatives. (In effect, their wages contain a rent component.) Clair Wilcox, one of the first economists to write on the subject of adjustment assistance, described the problem confronting government as follows:

'It is scarcely possible to make friends or influence people by telling them that you intend to take action that may put them out of business, destroy their jobs or reduce their incomes, even though you promise to take care of them by providing some sort of public assistance while they go through the agonies of adjustment... Business and labor do not want it. They would prefer to stay where they are, doing what they are doing and receiving the incomes they now enjoy.'[29]

Indeed, the possibility cannot be ignored that an announced policy of compensation for liberal trade would *intensify* the opposition to it by focussing public attention on the costs to the few, rather than the benefits to the many, of freer trade.

Such considerations suggest that the subsidy-equivalent of the bribe needed for a particular industry could be so large as to preclude it, for budgetary reasons, from being offered in the 'clean' lump-sum form assumed by many economists. (Note the collapse of the TAA programme in the United States once it lost its strict 'equity' rationale, described in Chapter 2.) The negotiated compensation is more likely to involve a package of measures, some of which will be chosen primarily for their budgetary convenience — like 'temporary' import restrictions, for instance. This, too, is confirmed by the actual experience with industry-specific adjustment schemes (textiles under the MFA).

The discussion so far has only taken into account the politically expedient approach within the confines of a single industry, at a given moment in time. But the compensation of one vested interest group in such a fashion must be expected to provoke demands for similar treatment from many other groups — both within the traded goods sector and outside it. Given an unprincipled expediency approach to government policy, it is worth everyone's while to flex their political muscles. In effect, the government is rewarding anti-social behaviour. Apart from the waste of productive resources to which this gives rise, the pressure upon governments would soon become unbearable because, under the assumptions on which the whole approach is based, they could not afford to resist.

NOTES AND REFERENCES

1. See, for example, Peter Henle, *Trade Adjustment Assistance for Workers: Issues of Program and Purpose* (Washington: Congressional Research Service, Library of Congress, 1976); Malcolm D. Bale, 'Adjustment Assistance: Dealing with Import-displaced Workers', in Walter Adams *et al*, *Tariffs, Quotas and Trade: the Politics of Protectionism* (San Fransisco: Institute for Contemporary Studies, 1979); Cprek, *op. cit.*; Leslie Stein, 'Trade Adjustment Assistance as a Means of Achieving Improved Resource Allocation through Freer Trade', *American Journal of Economics and Sociology*, Lancaster, Pennsylvania, July 1982.

2. Tracy Murray, *Adjustment Policies and the Need for an Early Warning Capability*, Paper presented to the International Symposium on 'Industrial Policies for the 80s', Madrid, 5-9 May 1980, p. 6.

3. For a detailed discussion about the true nature and policy relevance of externalities, see the seminal article by Ronald H. Coase, 'The Problem of Social Cost', *Journal of Law and Economics*, Chicago, October 1960. See also, Steven N.S. Cheung, *The Myth of Social Cost*, Hobart Paper No. 82 (London: Institute of Economic Affairs, 1978).

4. Arthur C. Pigou, *The Economics of Welfare* (London: Macmillan, 1920).

5. 'Policies for Adjustment: some General Orientations', in *Positive Adjustment Policies: Managing Structural Change, op. cit.*, p. 58. See also, H. Peter Gray, 'Senile Industry Protection: a Proposal', *Southern Economic Journal*, North Chapel, North Carolina, April 1973.

6. For an interesting attempt to argue the contrary, and a rebuttal of that argument, see Gray, *op. cit.*, and Geoffrey Wood, 'Senile Industry Protection: Comment', *Southern Economic Journal*, January 1975, respectively.

7. See Stephen P. Magee, "The Welfare Effects of Restrictions on US Trade', *Brookings Papers on Economic Activity*, Washington, No. 3, 1972; Robert E. Baldwin, John M. Mutti and J. David Richardson, 'Welfare Effects on the United States of a Significant Multilateral Tariff Reduction', *Journal of International Economics*, Amsterdam, August 1980.

8. Armen A. Alchian, 'Information Costs, Pricing and Resource Unemployment', *Western Economic Journal*, Los Angeles, June 1969.

9. These points can be illustrated with the following analogy. There is not just the possibility but a certainty that some minimum number of houses in a large city will burn down this year. That number could be reduced very sharply, perhaps to zero, by placing a fire station on every block. From the point of view of cost, however, that would be absurd. So each municipality tries to determine the least-cost combination of the three elements of social cost relevant in this case: (i) the probability that a house will burn down, (ii) the cost of the fire insurance that most members of the community will carry in the face of that probability and (iii) the cost of the public good of fire-fighting services. If, in this situation, the actuarially foreseen number of insured houses actually burns down, is it a social cost? The society is obviously poorer than it would have been if the houses had not burned down, but that is irrelevant. The point is that the cost of preventing their destruction (a fire station on every block) would have exceeded the value of the lost houses. Thus the fires inflict no cost on society apart from the private production cost of the insurance companies. Like house fires, unemployment is an insurable risk — that is, people are able to pool the risks of individual losses — and the pay-out on insurance claims obviously does not represent a social cost.

10. This insight was expressed by an experienced civil servant to one of the authors as follows: 'Only too often it is not imports that cause 'injury' but prior injury that attracts imports.'

11. See, Harold Demsetz, 'Information and Efficiency: another Viewpoint', *Journal of Law and Economics*, April 1969.

12. For example, it has been argued that, 'ideally, it might be best to eliminate the market imperfection causing resource immobility. But, in practice, trade adjustment schemes present

themselves as useful second-best instruments, even though they might degenerate into social insurance programmes for the inefficient.' Stein, 'Measures to Assist Adjustments to Freer Trade', *American Journal of Economics and Sociology*, July 1983, p. 324.

13. See J. Peter Neary, 'Intersectoral Capital Mobility, Wage Stickiness and the Case for Adjustment Assistance', and Michael Mussa, 'Government Policy and the Adjustment Process', besides other contributions to Jagdish N. Bhagwati (ed.), *Import Competition and Response* (Chicago and London: University of Chicago Press, for the National Bureau of Economic Research, 1982).

14. Michael McKee and Edwin G. West, 'The Theory of the Second Best: a Solution in Search of a Problem', *Economic Inquiry*, Los Angeles, July 1981, p. 447.

15. As presented in the models of Michael Bruno, Michael Mussa and Neary in Bhagwati (ed.), *op. cit.*

16. Harry G. Johnson's famous dictum comes to mind:

'The fundamental problem is that, as with all second-best arguments, determination of the conditions under which a second-best policy actually leads to an improvement of social welfare requires detailed theoretical and empirical investigation by a first-best economist. Unfortunately, policy is generally formulated by fourth-best economists and administered by third-best economists; it is therefore very unlikely that a second-best welfare optimum will result from policies based on second-best arguments.'

17. See, among others, Frank, *op. cit.*, Murray, *op. cit.*; and C. Michael Aho and Thomas O. Bayard, 'Costs and Benefits of Trade Adjustment Assistance', Paper presented at a conference convened by the National Bureau of Economic Research on the Structure and Evolution of Recent US Trade Policy, Cambridge, Massachusetts, 3-4 December 1982.

18. See Gordon Tullock, 'The Transitional Gains Trap', *Bell Journal of Economics*, New York, Autumn 1975.

19. Harold M. Hochman, 'Rule Change and Transitional Equity', in Hochman and G.E. Peterson (eds), *Redistribution Through Public Choice* (New York: Columbia University Press, 1974). Note that Hochman, too, uses 'costs' interchangeably with 'wealth losses'. There could only be a *true* cost from rule changes if they adversely affected production incentives. Mr Hochman recognizes this when he writes later of 'demoralization costs' (p. 327). But in the case of trade liberalization, the rule changes are more likely to be salutary

in their effect on production incentives, by reducing rent-seeking and moral hazard; that is, the 'demoralization' effect would be focussed on *un*productive activity.

20. See Stanley D. Metzger, 'The Escape Clause and Adjustment Assistance: Proposals and Assessments', *Law and Policy in International Business*, Summer 1970.

21. See, among others, Peter J. Lloyd, *Non-tariff Distortions of Australian Trade* (Canberra: Australian National University Press, 1973); Wolf, *op. cit.*; Neary, *op. cit.*; and also Aho and Bayard, 'American Trade Adjustment Assistance after Five Years', *The World Economy*, London, November 1980, where it is observed:

'In the real world where political and distributional questions often dominate efficiency considerations, a second-best and admittedly distortionary compensation policy may be considerably more efficient as a government response to interest-group lobbying than a third-best policy of increased trade restrictions.'

22. This obviously does not hold as a *general* proposition. There are numerous examples of governments refusing protection without resorting to other assistance.

23. Immanuel Kant, *On the Old Saw: That May be Right in Theory, but it Won't Work in Practice* (Pittsburg: University of Pennsylvania, 1974).

24. Peter G. Warr, 'The Case Against Tariff Compensation', *The Australian Journal of Agricultural Economics*, August 1978, p. 88.

25. For a detailed discussion, see Clarence Philbrook, 'Realism in Policy Espousal', *American Economic Review*, December 1953.

26. Warr, *loc. cit.*

27. William H. Hutt, *Politically Impossible...?* (London: Institute of Economic Affairs, 1971).

28. See H.G. Johnson, 'Forward', in Denton, O'Cleireacain and Ash, *op. cit.*; Bale, in Adams *et al*, *op. cit.*; Graham Glenday, Glenn P. Jenkins and John C. Evans, 'Worker Adjustment to Liberalized Trade', Staff Working Paper No. 426 (Washington: World Bank, 1980); Aho and James Orr, *Demographic and Occupational Characteristic of Workers in Trade-sensitive Industries*, Economic Discussion Paper No. 2 (Washington: US Department of Labor, April 1980).

29. Clair Wilcox, 'Relief for Victims of Tariffs Cuts', *American Economic Review*, December 1950, p. 885. The same point is made by Dean Hinton, 'Comment: Policy Issues', in Hughes, *op. cit.*, who also notes: 'This really becomes binding when we look at it

from the level of the union leadership. If union members move, the leader does not have a union, he does not have a dues check-off, he does not have anything; this is one reason why I presume Nat Goldfinger [an American trade union leader] talked about adjustment assistance as a burial program or some such phrase.'

Chapter 4

Public Assistance and Private Incentives

'The most disquieting effect of the tariff has been the stimulus it has given to demands for government assistance of all kinds, with the consequent demoralizing effect on self-reliant efficiency throughout all forms of production'

— J.B. Brigden *et al.*, *The Australian Tariff: an Economic Enquiry*, Brigden Report (1929)

FISCAL THEORY and policy devote considerable effort to analysing the impact on economic behaviour of the announcement, or even the expectation, of a new tax. Such a tax represents an important new datum which forces a re-arrangement of the existing plans of all economic agents affected. The policy-maker needs to know whether this re-arrangement will on balance foster or hinder the kinds of economic activity which in his view promote social welfare. This consideration has an equally important place in the discussion of adjustment assistance and industrial policy in general. If they are to be efficient, they must take into account the changes in the behaviour of firms, industry associations and labour unions which will result from the knowledge that government intends to intervene.

Public subsidy programmes for producer groups have effects on production incentives which may cost a country far more than the administrative costs of the programmes. Yet an awareness of these costs is typically absent from the literature recommending government action to 'improve' the adjustment process or 'promote' industrial development. Instead, it is normally assumed that subsidy payments of this kind 'represent a transfer and therefore are not a social cost'.[1] This chapter considers two ways in which such transfers can give rise to social costs.

MORAL HAZARD

First, there is the issue which insurance theory labels 'moral hazard'. The fact of being insured against a particular kind of accident may so alter the behaviour of the insured person as actually to increase the probability of that accident happening. (For example, someone insured against theft may become less careful in locking the apartment.) The intangible, loss-producing propensities of individuals and enterprises are triggered off by insurance against loss. Since all the industry-oriented forms of adjustment policy entail insurance against the rigours of the market, the problem of 'moral hazard' assumes some importance.

An industry experiencing pressure from imports can, if left to its own devices, adjust only by innovating. It will abandon certain lines of production and concentrate on improving others, trying to offer some additional quality or service to distinguish its own product from the imported one. In this effort it can be aided by its own labour force, which will adapt its wage-bargaining strategy to the perceived danger of the industry's market, and *a fortiori* its employment, shrinking in consequence of comparative advantage shifting against it. Indeed, the rate of change in comparative advantage can be to a considerable extent controlled by the import-competing industry, since its competitive position *vis-à-vis* foreign suppliers is largely determined by the relation between the growth of the money wages it pays and of the labour productivity it generates.

If public subsidies are used to promote the withdrawal of productive factors from the industry under import pressure, it is likely that some of the innovations which otherwise would have been made will not occur. Two reasons are that subsidies for the scrapping of capital installations will reduce the pressure on enterprise and management, and that the availability of additional benefits to workers made redundant by imports will influence the bargaining strategy of unions in the import-competing industries. At the limit, if the government guaranteed domestic industry a fixed share of the domestic market, there would be no way to control the industry's wages — and thus the wage level in general, since industries pay active attention to their wage relativities.

A special problem arises in those situations where the government provides finance at less-than-market rates for specific projects. In principle, the best test of the commercial viability of such projects is the terms on which the necessary finance can be obtained from the capital market. Commercial finance is almost always obtainable, but on conditions of varying severity. Even the most radical solutions that the institutions of the capital market devise in cases of industrial failure — solutions such as takeover, reorganization or even receivership and liquidation — are instruments of adjustment. They are essentially accounting operations involving a correction of book values; their purpose is to secure better management for socially-valuable real assets.[2] They all begin to operate on the perception of a discrepancy between the book value, or actual market value, and the *potential* market value of the enterprise in difficulty. Takeover incentive is provided by the realization that the present management is not getting out of the existing assets all that they are capable of yielding. There is a continuum between less-than-maximum profits and actual losses. When there are large losses and debts there is no longer an incentive for a takeover. The alert entrepeneur, perceiving the higher earnings potential of the assets in question, may discuss a 'consolidation' with the main parties involved, this being a form of privately-agreed bankruptcy. Otherwise, he will wait until after bankruptcy proceedings, assuming control of the assets only after they have been purged of debt.

Government-sponsored financial salvage schemes to avert bankruptcy (provision of capital, credit guarantees) have two effects, both undesirable.

First, they generally serve to sustain the existing management under whose stewardship the crisis occurred. Government finance will always be preferred by the management to the otherwise available private finance, because the conditions and supervision entailed in the latter would be more stringent.

Second, the injections of general taxpayers money serve to reduce the losses of those private investors who hold the equity of the enterprise. By contrast, when a salvage plan is devised by the financial institutions of the market, the risks are, properly, borne by the holders of equity.

Another important difference between the 'salvage plans' of government and the market is that the latter will always be self-terminating. Financial institutions know the point at which they must cut their losses, and stop throwing good money after bad, whereas the government will generally continue to do so far beyond this point. Being aware that it embodies social authority, government finds it difficult to admit mistakes. It may need an acute political crisis to be able to cut off its support to lame ducks.

Finally, assistance to the 'growth sectors' or 'sunrise industries' could be the most counter-productive of all. The firms through which industrial progress is unfolding do not need public assistance. They can obtain from private sources all the capital they can handle. Offering them more capital at subsidized rates of interest is not only unnecessary, it could actually be harmful. This is an area of enterprise where the failure rate is inevitably (and necessarily) very high. Public assistance to such firms — socialization of risk — would give them an incentive to take risks that would otherwise not be taken. Premature expansion of such firms would entail a dilution of their main asset, management capacity.

RENT SEEKING

A second important way in which transfers create cost is through the diversion of resources (especially managerial expertise) from productive activities to lobbying government.

This activity is perfectly rational for profit-seeking enterprises operating in an institutional environment which includes the possibility of government assistance. The 'investment' in lobbying will continue to the point where its expected returns have declined to the level derivable from alternative activities. From a firm's point of view, it makes no difference from which source its profits flow, as long as they are maximized in aggregate. From society's viewpoint, however, it matters a great deal, for lobbying activity, by contrast to the alternative uses to which the firm's resources may be put, generates no social product. It has to do with the distribution of national income, not with its creation. To distinguish it from other, productive, forms of profit-making activity, lobbying has been called *rent seeking*, which has been described as 'behaviour in institutional settings where individual efforts to maximize value generate social waste rather than social surplus'.[3]

The rising importance of rent-seeking activity to the private sector is demonstrated by the shift in the composition of managerial staff of even relatively small corporations from people with technical skills relevant to the industry in question in favour of lawyers.[4] It is also apparent in the many industry associations and in the growth of small consultancy businesses, the activities of which are entirely concerned with lobbying (preparation of submissions for their clients as well as more discreet ways of influencing the political decision-making process).

The cost to a society of rent-seeking depends on how easy it is to obtain government assistance. At one extreme, one can imagine a country with a constitutional prohibition on selective public assistance to industry interests. In such a country there would be no resources wasted in lobbying government. The return on any such use of resources would be known to be zero. Once there is the possibility of government intervention, however, the amount of rent-seeking will be determined by expectations, which will in turn be largely based on the actual policy experience. For example, in another country, assistance may have been given only in precisely-specified situations, following an exhaustive legislative discussion and majority agreement about its objects and means. In these circumstances, too, there would probably not be much rent-seeking, for special-interest groups would soon learn that proposals to reassign income to them at the cost of other groups would meet opposition within the legislature. The expectation of obtaining rents would be relatively low.

A third situation, corresponding more nearly to present reality, is that of a 'flexible' government approach towards selective public assistance. At certain times, the emphasis may have favoured different categories of claimant and the legislative history may have been a varied one, with a considerable degree of discretionary power being exercised by the executive. It should be clear that in this situation the probability of successful lobbying will be relatively high and many groups will have an incentive to participate. Lobbying activity will be devoted (i) to increasing the benefits to existing recipients and (ii) to extending assistance to other groups (or opposing such an extension). It will be directed both at the political process and at the administration.

The magnitude of the cost of rent-seeking will now depend on the magnitude of the expected transfers. It will also depend on how selective are those transfers. For example, a large-scale re-distribution of income effected through income tax may be very great in the aggregate, but not give rise to much lobbying activity because the groups involved are too large to form an effective coalition.[5] When the size of the group, though, is such that the expected cost or benefit per member of the group becomes quite large, members will be more likely to form a coalition for lobbying purposes or even to lobby individually.

It could be argued that the very inactivity of the large, unorganized groups of taxpayers and consumers bearing the burden of industrial support would reduce the need for much lobbying effort by the industry concerned. But the competition is generally not between those who pay for, and those who receive, the transfers; it is mostly among those on the 'demand' side of this equation, assistance being a scarce good. There are a number of ways of seeing this. If all public assistance is budgetary, then obviously there is a limit in aggregate and industries must compete for shares of the pie. But the same applies to border protection. Not every industry can be protected: the true level of protection to one is determined by the protection received by the others.[6]

In circumstances of vigorous competition for public assistance, it has been shown that the cost of rent-seeking will tend to approach the value of the rent itself.[7] If so, the cost of transfers could amount to a large multiple of the deadweight loss associated with market divergences and distortions.[8]

NOTES AND REFERENCES

1. Aho and Bayard, 'American Trade Adjustment Assistance after Five Years', *loc. cit.*, p. 361. They add: 'Thus the TAA programme looks like a fairly good investment.'

2. On the economic significance of 'enterprise failure', see John Burton, *Picking Losers? The Political Economy of Industrial Policy*, Hobart Paper No. 99 (London: Institute for Economic Affairs, 1983).

See also Lloyd, 'A Knightian Model for the Analysis of Structural Adjustments by Firms', *Weltwirtschaftliches Archiv*, Kiel, No. 4, Vol. 117, 1981, where it is noted:

'It is important to appreciate that a given change ... will have different effects on different firms... Firms which are more risk-averse or less flexible in their ability to change production will make fewer responses to adverse developments and they will be slower to take advantage of new market opportunities... If this relatively slow response is due to greater risk aversion or less perceptive management there is no justification for government assistance which allows these troubled firms to stay in production... One desirable part of structural adjustment is that these firms and the resources they employ be absorbed by other firms. The disappearance of some firms from the market-place occurs continually and is as desirable as the emergence of new firms' (p. 683).

3. James H. Buchanan, 'Rent Seeking and Profit Seeking', in Buchanan, Robert D. Tollison and Tullock (eds), *Toward a Theory*

of the Rent-seeking Society (College Station: Texas A and M University
Press, 1980) p. 4. Also see Tollison, 'Rent Seeking: a Survey',
Kyklos, Basle, Vol. 35, 1982.
    4. Tullock, 'Rent-seeking as a Negative-sum Game', in
Buchanan, Tollison and Tullock, *op. cit.*
    5. See the exchange between Gordon Tullock and Edgar K.
Browning in Buchanan, Tollison and Tullock, *op. cit.*, pp. 283-92.
    6. For a detailed discussion, see Kenneth Clements and Larry
A. Sjaastad, *How Protection Taxes Exporters*, Thames Essay No. 39
(London: Trade Policy Research Centre, 1984).
    7. Anne Krueger, 'The Political Economy of the Rent-seeking
Society', *American Economic Review*, June 1974.
    8. For this reason, a switch from border protection to subsidies
could conceivably *increase* the welfare cost of public assistance to
industries; that is to say, the rent-seeking costs of a subsidy-support
system could exceed those with border protection by more than the
value of the deadweight loss due to the price distortion. Compared
with tariffs, a subsidy system is characterized by greater
administrative discretion, periodic review of public assistance and
scope for firm-specific aids, all of which will induce greater lobbying
efforts. Against this, a subsidy system would soon run into a budget
constraint, whereas the (partly offsetting) re-distribution effected
through tariffs would not.

Chapter 5

Impediments to the Adjustment Process of the Market

'We cannot possibly afford *perfect* markets, but we regulate real markets in many ways and it would be desirable to know what these regulations are achieving'

— George J. Stigler, 'Imperfections in the Capital Market', *Journal of Political Economy*, Chicago, June 1967

ADJUSTMENT is an exercise in foresight. Market pressures make certain activities unprofitable; new and better uses for the factors of production released from such activities have to be sought, imagined, created. This need for foresight is often invoked by governments to justify 'anticipatory adjustment policy', the promotion of 'sunrise industries' *et cetera*. Nevertheless, government cannot exercise, on behalf of industry, the detailed foresight needed for anticipating which particular lines of production will eventually have to be abandoned and which will grow. The decentralized institutions of the market search for and make use of the information needed for this purpose much more effectively than governments could ever be expected to do.[1] The problem is that the quality of the information on which they depend has deteriorated.

The information needed for adjustment is conveyed by changes in relative prices: the price system is essentially an information-processing mechanism.[2] It coordinates the diverse, changing desires and constraints of a myriad of individuals on the supply and demand sides of the markets that make up an economy. The information conveyed by the price system is of greatest value when national prices have been connected into an *international price system* by liberal international trade and investment, in conjunction with international monetary arrangements providing for free convertibility of the major currencies. Changes in the relative prices formed in such a competitive international market transmit promptly, throughout the world economy, information about shortages and surpluses incipient in any part of it. Indeed, since these prices reflect the expectations of a large number of market participants, they often *anticipate* the volume changes and thus serve to reduce their eventual magnitude. The existence of an international price system makes it possible for firms to plan their adjustment and thus accomplish it without major dislocation.[3]

If there is a need, then, for something called 'adjustment policy', it must be concerned above all with achieving a well-functioning price system, one that is responsive to those underlying changes in the world economy which create the need (and opportunity) for adjustment and growth itself. An adjustment policy can be efficient only when it supports the international price system.[4]

This emphasis on the information function of the price system transcends the economist's traditional theoretic concern with static market failure. That concern was limited to those special situations (externalities, public goods, natural monopoly) in which a *free market* would fail to produce goods in the 'right' quantities. But present-day markets are characterised by an absence of freedom. The majority of market 'failures', in the informational sense, could be said to result from *impediments* to the proper functioning of markets. It is these sources of failure — in labour, capital and product markets — that are the main concern of this chapter.

LABOUR MARKETS

Much adjustment policy has involved measures to promote the occupational and regional mobility of labour. The main focus has been on re-training and 're-location' subsidies of one sort or another. In many cases, however, such interventions in the labour market have not proved a success, especially those intended to promote the regional mobility of labour.[5] This is unsurprising, for most people derive considerable utility from living in their home region, in the same way that they derive utility from any consumption good. If the satisfactory functioning of a competitive economy depended on raising labour's regional mobility, there would be little cause for hope.[6] By contrast to capital, labour is inherently a regionally immobile factor of production, especially in the lower-skilled categories, and economic theory allows for this fact. (Note that the theory of foreign trade *assumes* labour to be immobile between countries.) With sufficient flexibility of relative wages, labour need not move, capital will come to it. The main problem in labour markets is precisely that relative wages have become increasingly rigid. In addition, in most countries there exists a range of measures that are equivalent in their effects to a *tax* on labour mobility.

Restrictive Practices

It is well known that the predominant source of wage rigidity in contemporary economies is the restrictive practices of trade unions. As an impediment to adjustment and growth, however, it is not the 'monopoly pricing' of labour in itself which poses the main problem. Enterprises eventually adjust to increased labour costs by substituting capital for labour. The effect is thus simply higher unemployment than would otherwise exist, but not necessarily reduced growth. (Monopoly wage-setting by unions is mainly a vehicle for *re-distributing* income within the labour force: the associated unemployment is predominantly borne by non-union and less productive labour.[7]) The more serious, growth-impeding, features of labour unions are

(a) wage demands maintaining *fixed wage relativities* between different skills and industries, and

(b) *neo-Luddism*, the outright resistance to new technology and conditions imposed on its use.

When relative wages do not respond to shifts in the pattern of demand for labour among industries and regions, 'structural' unemployment is inevitable. The redirection of labour in sufficient numbers from lower to higher productivity uses requires the existence of wage differentials that provide an incentive to move. The co-existence of skill shortages with high unemployment in a number of countries in recent years shows that wage structures have not provided such an incentive — that the price signals have been wrong. Similarly, the existence of relatively high levels of unemployment in regions where the old-established industries have lost competitiveness, is largely due to nation-wide wage fixing, which prevents the decline in relative wages in these regions that is needed to slow down industrial decline and attract new investment.[8]

The extent to which unions are successful in blocking market adjustment depends on the degree of their monopoly power. This in turn partly depends on their ability to impede competition within the domestic labour force. The experience among countries is quite varied in this respect, depending on their special historical, social and legal circumstances. In all of them, there are considerable political obstacles to *direct* government action to increase competition within the labour force. Most countries do have laws addressing some of the sources of the coercive power of the labour unions (note the recent legislation in the United Kingdom), but none seem likely to be able to pass the most needed reform, namely an anti-trust law for labour unions, confining their effective organization to the level of individual firms.

There is another important source of labour union power which is often overlooked. Labour unions depend to a large extent on the ability of enterprises to pass on, or be compensated for, the higher costs of their restrictive practices. Demands by labour unions tend to be most intransigent in industries which are 'sheltered' by nationalization, regulation or protection. As Gottfried Haberler, of the American Enterprise Institute in Washington, has observed in a recent essay: 'Unions know, or find out quickly, that striking against world markets is risky. This is the reason why in small countries where international trade is a large fraction of the economy, labour unions are usually much more reasonable.'[9] The multiple role of import restrictions in impeding the adjustment process is a theme which will be taken up again later.

Minimum-wage Legislation

Minimum-wage laws were passed long ago in a number of countries with the intention of preventing the exploitation of youths and minority groups and ensuring all workers a minimum standard of living. The perverse effects of these laws (or equivalent measures imposed by unions) have become widely known.[10] From an adjustment perspective, the main problem is not just that they reduce the total demand for low-skilled or less productive labour, but that they also discriminate against

(a) those industries which use greater proportions of low-skilled labour (such as textiles, clothing and footwear, three industries which epitomise the 'adjustment problem' in contemporary economies) and

(b) those regions in decline which need to attract new investment through lower labour costs.

Note that when the demand for certain skills declines, the re-employment of the displaced workers will require some transitional 'learning' on their part. This would normally be provided by a new employer at a wage which (temporarily) reflected the lower value of the newcomer's labour. Minimum wages can prevent this adjustment mechanism from operating. Similarly, the problem of youth unemployment is largely attributable to minimum-wage legislation.[11] In Switzerland, where on-the-job training is widely provided at wages considerably below those for skilled workers, the rate of youth unemployment is only marginally greater than that for the rest of the workforce (and all unemployment is very low).[12]

A mandated wage which is common to new entrants to the work force and those with previous experience alike, will obviously discriminate against the former group. This is tacitly recognized by the attempt of some governments, through special youth-training programmes, to raise the quality of young workers to a level which corresponds to the wage that they legally must be paid. Minimum-wage and equal-wage rules have also been found to increase rates of unemployment for certain minority and racial groups, as well as for women. As has been argued, 'in a purely informational sense, the employer still knows low productivity or high-risk categories of workers, but that only insures that the lack of *effective* knowledge transmission through prices (wages) will lead to less employment of them'.[13]

Job 'Security' Requirements

Many countries now have laws and regulations, including agreements through collective bargaining, which severely constrain the demand side of the labour market. Employers are variously obliged (i) to give lengthy notification of dismissals, (ii) to negotiate the conditions of such dismissals with government representatives, (iii) to pay substantial severance compensation, (iv) to find alternative employment for redundant workers and (v) even to recruit their workers from approved lists held by government employment agencies.[14]

While such measures are often placed under the banner of 'adjustment policy', they obviously not only weaken the adjustment capacity of enterprises (forcing some into bankruptcy as the only way of avoiding such obligations) but also reduce the *effective* 'security' of labour in two ways:

(a) by raising its cost and encouraging employers to switch to less labour-intensive techniques of production; and

(b) by discriminating against those without a job (including, again, first-time entrants into the labour force).

As the eminent New Zealand economist, A.G.B. Fisher, observed in 1945:

'We need to distinguish with the utmost sharpness between stability for an economy as a whole, with individuals from time to time changing their places in it, and the situation which would develop if we extended indefinitely the process of securing to each individual the job which he already happened to have. The former is consistent with both progress and security; the latter, if universally applied, would make progress of any kind quite impossible, and security in the end highly improbable.'[15]

The adjustment process depends on a high 'natality rate' of enterprises. Recent research in the United States has shown that the major source of the vast number of new jobs created in that country has been small enterprises with few employees and low overheads.[16] Such firms operate in a high-risk environment where flexibility in decision-making is essential and premature mortality common. Many such enterprises would never have been conceived had they been obliged to meet the job-security requirements that are prevalent in Western Europe, the cumulative effect of which has been to convert labour into another fixed factor of production. In so far as such requirements make it difficult to correct entrepreneurial error by discontinuing unpromising lines of production, they reduce not only the effective mobility of labour and capital but also the growth of the capital stock and the economy as a whole.

The Social Security and Taxation Trap

Once a taboo subject, even for academic research, a number of detailed studies are now appearing which confirm that unemployment benefits combined with low income-tax thresholds can effectively eliminate the incentive for low-skilled workers to seek (re-)employment, once the value of their leisure time is accounted for.[17] This has undoubtedly played some part in the rising proportion of 'long-term unemployed' and the higher so-called 'natural' rate of unemployment observed in several countries. Similarly, the provision of 'social housing' at subsidized rates is a major disincentive for redundant workers to search for or accept employment outside their home region, compounding the effect of rigid wages on regionally-concentrated unemployment.

CAPITAL MARKETS

The capital market is the knowledge and information-processing centre of a free-enterprise economy. Its prime function is asset valuation. More precisely, it is concerned with valuing the specific combinations and interactions of physical and human assets manifested in different entrepreneurial activities or 'enterprises'. The worth of an enterprise is the discounted value of its foreseeable future net earnings. These have to be guessed at in the light of knowledge and information available at the moment. Since knowledge of this kind is always changing, capital values must constantly fluctuate.

Because the discovery of relevant new information tends to be highly rewarded, the capital market is ruthlessly concerned with searching for and evaluating such information. It is a highly-competitive environment in which 'mistakes' cannot endure and (by contrast to government) vested interests in obsolete information cannot be formed.[18] As in other markets, the capital market could never be 'perfect', in the sense of acting on perfect knowledge. Indeed, it is the very existence of risk and uncertainty in economic life which provides its *raison d'être*: it is the best and clearest window on the economic future a society has.

It has already been noted that capital is on the whole much more mobile than labour. Capital is a stock having a continuous outflow (depreciation) and inflow (new investment). These *financial* flows are the means by which capital 'adjusts' to changes in the conditions of demand and supply. They are the sources of its 'mobility' — in the only sense in which capital mobility matters. When people speak of capital immobility, they are usually referring to the machinery and equipment on the factory floors of troubled firms. In this physical form, of course, capital is relatively immobile (although factory buildings have many uses and much machinery is basic to several industries[19]), but this is of no economic importance. What is important is that the physical capital in use at a given moment is socially productive, not that it operates for its own sake.

Sometimes the inability of certain projects to obtain adequate finance is taken to be evidence of shortcomings or 'failure' in the capital market.[20] What needs to be demonstrated, however, is that, given the limited supply of capital available and the competing demands for its use, the projects in question should have received *precedence* over others. There are reasons why a 'mis-ordering' can take place, but they are generally not intrinsic to the capital market itself.[21]

Taxation

In no industrial country is the taxation system neutral in its effects on resource allocation; in most, its effects are extremely complex, with many offsetting provisions. Given the tax laws as they are — for example, the income tax code in the United States is over 2,000 pages long, the Internal Revenue Service's interpretive regulations an additional several hundred thousand pages — it is impossible to know which investments are intrinsically (socially) profitable and which are being pursued only for tax reasons. For example, in the United States, the average *effective* rates of taxation (after allowances) on gross corporate income were recently estimated to vary from 2 per cent in telecommunications and 6 per cent in insurance to 39 per cent in the rubber industry. The incidence of taxation among different sized corporations was also shown to vary widely, with the largest burden falling on 'middle-size' companies.[22] Similarly, in the United Kingdom, it was recently calculated that the post-tax rate of return on an investment that yields a pre-tax return of 10 per cent, could range from 1.7 per cent to 25 per cent.[23]

There is evidence that levels of taxation on productive activities in general have now become so high that a bias has been created favouring consumption over investment, with savings being increasingly channelled into consumer durables, 'collectibles' and real estate. The interaction of the tax system with inflation has greatly encouraged such a shift since the mid-1970s.[24]

Regulation

Other impediments to the efficient functioning of capital and credit markets are (i) government regulations which segment and restrict entry to these markets and (ii) controls on rates of interest.

Barriers to entry are extremely difficult to organize and enforce in capital markets without government support because 'capital is the most fungible, the most divisible, the most mobile of all productive resources'.[25] This support has in many countries been forthcoming under the guise of preventing 'destructive competition' or protecting the interests of small savers. Governments have (i) restricted access to the general banking sector, (ii) separated the functions of different financial institutions to prevent internal competition and (iii) regulated or assisted the self-regulation of the stock exchanges,[26] *et cetera*... As in other markets, monopolistic practices serve to raise the *price* of the product (finance) and reduce the *volume* of transactions.

At the same time, however, governments have placed ceilings on rates of interest, either generally or, more often, for particular classes of transactions, such as savings accounts and home mortgages. The effect of interest-rate controls in financial markets is analogous to that of minimum-wage laws in labour markets. Interest-rate ceilings reduce the supply of capital in their area of application and discriminate within these categories in favour of higher 'quality' (more dependable) borrowers. Normally, financial institutions will not discriminate against riskier investments in the sense of not making funds available, but they will require a higher rate of interest on such lending to bring the expected rate of return up to the level obtainable from projects with less possibility of default.

Inflation

The restrictive and distorting effects of interest-rate controls are heightened in inflationary times. More generally, inflation affects the allocation of capital in three ways.[27]

1. Inflation reduces the overall *level* of investment demand. It does this both by raising the level of uncertainty about future streams of income, thus increasing the riskiness of a given investment project, and, in conjunction with a system of taxation in which depreciation deductions are based on the 'historical cost' of physical capital, by reducing after-tax profitability of investment.

2. Inflation affects the *timing* of investment. Under stable price levels, the coordination of individual economic decisions and plans is achieved by relative prices, the changes in which indicate where shortages are emerging and additional investment is needed. In the process of inflation, most prices are repeatedly adjusted upwards, but each with a different lag. Consequently, the pattern of relative prices existing at any moment conveys little useful information on which to base production and investment decisions. This loss of vital information would occur even if investors were able to anticipate perfectly increases in the general level of prices. As a result, with each percentage point of real growth, new bottlenecks appear, which in normal circumstances relative price changes would have made it possible to foresee and avoid.

3. Inflation affects the *composition*, and thus the efficiency, of investment by skewing it towards short-lived assets, in particular towards machinery and equipment as against new plant. This occurs for two reasons.

First, risk increases with the project's useful life: the further into the future a given net income flow must be projected, the less predictable or more risky it will be.

Second, the combined effects of inflation and depreciation based on historical cost will ensure that the short-term project will be preferred, even if investors are assumed to have perfect foresight about future income. This is because, under such a system, the tax savings from depreciation always remain the same in nominal terms. With inflation the real value of these tax savings falls and this decline is greater for longer write-off periods. Since long-term investment, such as investment in plant, is an important element in the process of structural change, the fact that inflation biases investment decisions against such projects is clearly an added impediment to adjustment.

Product Markets

Finally, the discussion turns to product markets. The impediments in product markets have become so pervasive in recent times that it seems justified to enquire:

'What *remains* of the price system?... Government services, now a substantial part of total output everywhere, are clearly not priced by the spontaneous interplay of supply and demand. The bulk of agricultural output is marketed at prices set by the political process. Textiles and clothing, industries with vigorous internal competition, are effectively sheltered against low-cost foreign competition in most countries while steel, without significant competition at national level, is also extensively regulated in international trade. Shipbuilding in industrial countries continues to exist only by virtue of subsidies. Energy supply, subject to non-competitive pricing, has been a major source of instability. Petrochemicals are largely cartelized, the world's most efficient producer of automobiles is severely constrained in foreign trade, extensive international political negotiations are going on about where and under what conditions the latest technological innovations will be produced, and most services (such as transportation, insurance and communications) are both politically regulated and protected against import competition.'[28]

Monopoly Power

Although monopoly is one of the classic forms of 'market failure', three generations of economists have been unable to agree whether an active anti-monopoly policy is at all necessary. What seems clear, however, is that the social cost of monopoly (the 'welfare loss') is determined by the efficacy of *barriers* to entering an industry, not by the number of firms.[29] Competition laws designed to prevent any takeovers which would increase industry concentration beyond some arbitrary level frequently only serve to protect less efficient firms and their managements from competition itself.[30]

From an adjustment perspective, cartels — groups of sellers who undertake to share markets among themselves — are much more of a liability than the textbook cases of single-firm or natural monopoly. The latter type is a single decision-maker and, provided that it is an 'open' monopoly without government protection, it will normally be quite flexible in its response to changing market conditions.[31] By contrast, cartels are complex decision-making organizations. Decisions are made by a group of entrepreneurs with different preferences and constraints, each of whom attempts to maximize the interests of his own firm in any given change in cartel 'policy'. This makes change and reaction to change within the cartel difficult. For such reasons, cartels are observed to have 'sticky' prices and to be slow to innovate.[32] Another way of describing the difference is to say that the social cost cartels has an inherent tendency to grow over time, reducing the *rate of growth* of the economy at large, whereas that from natural monopolies does not.

In the absence of government support, all forms of monopoly share an extreme difficulty in conserving market power. Cartels not only must prevent entry, or ensure that

any entrants are also signed up, there is always the danger
of an existing member cheating on the cartel or leaving it
altogether, attracted by the profits to be derived from under-
cutting its price. In addition to these domestic threats, national
monopolies in traded goods and services face a much greater
threat from foreign suppliers. Where international trade is
liberal, it becomes necessary to cartelize all sellers, not just
domestic producers, and this is a considerable obstacle to their
effective operation.

The policy problem presented by cartels is also reduced by
the fact that, by contrast to monopoly power which may be
associated with concentration, the existence of cartels is a
clearly justiciable issue. All that is required is a judgment as
to whether independent firms have, or have not, agreed among
themselves to fix prices, divide markets or reduce supply. But
this side of competition law, where it exists, has tended to
be neglected[33] or actually flouted by government itself.
Governments have promoted cartels of the following kinds:

Regulated service cartels, such as professional services
(medicine, law), domestic transport (taxis) and air
travel.[34]

'Crisis' industry cartels, in combination with protection
from imports, such as steel and synthetic fibres in the
European Community and shipbuilding in Japan.[35]

Domestic agricultural cartels, which include price-support
schemes and 'right-to-produce' quota allocations, for
several products in North America, Western Europe and
elsewhere.[36]

International commodity cartels, explicit inter-governmental
cartels among producers, such as the Organization of
Petroleum Exporting Countries (OPEC) or implicit ones
including consumers, such as coffee, rubber *et cetera*.[37]

Export-restraint cartels, organized by governments (such
as Japan) to implement export restraint agreements with
importing countries or, internationally, orderly marketing
arrangements which essentially cartelize the suppliers to

protected markets (steel to the European Community, textiles and clothing under the MFA).

Protectionism

An analysis of monopoly power clearly overlaps with the issue of protectionism. If protectionist measures were to be ranked according to their long-term potential for impeding adjustment and growth, one could begin with a hierarchy of three categories:

1. At the bottom, are *subsidies*. This is not just because they do less violence to the price system than other forms of protection, but also because the recurring need to finance them, through the budget, acts as a constraint on how far a government can go in this direction. (That is why subsidy programmes are usually dependent on border protection, Europe's Common Agriculture Policy being a case in point.)

2. In the next place are *tariffs*, because (i) they create a once-for-all wedge between domestic and world prices and do not interfere thereafter with the normal functioning of the price system and (ii) they have price effects which are relatively transparent; in other words, nominal tariffs face political ceilings. Nevertheless, they also have some political disadvantages compared with subsidies. The tariff is a semi-permanent arrangement giving rise to quasi-property rights. Reinforcing the staying power of tariffs is the fact that, from the point of view of governments, they are devices which earn revenue, whereas subsidies absorb it.

3. But the top place in the hierarchy of protectionist impediments to adjustment must be awarded to *quantitative* import restrictions, for they do maximum violence to the price system — indeed, they can paralyse the price system in their areas of application — yet are least constrained by political pressure, because their price and income-redistribution effects are not as readily discernible. By contrast to (bound) tariffs, the price distortions caused by quantitative restrictions (and hence the cost to the importing country) grow over time as a country loses comparative advantage.[38]

The cost of quantitative restrictions is minimized, however, when they take the form of global quotas, with licences to import being sold in a public auction.[39] Importers remain free to choose the least-cost sources of supply and no exporting country can complain of being discriminated against. Three important consequences ensue.

First, the importing country (if not the private consumers or users) obtains its total imports of the restricted product at the lowest cost, foreign exporters having to compete for orders under the quota.

Thus, second, only prices in the importing country will be distorted, as international prices will still reflect the true scarcity value of the products in question (after adjustment to the imposition of the quota).

Finally, the prices of import licences formed in the auction reflect the margin of protection; as a result, domestic political discussion is better informed and, as in the case of tariffs, the margin of protection is captured for public revenue.

The *most* costly form of quantitative restriction is that which is negotiated and administered in the form of the so-called 'voluntary' export-restraint agreements.[40] Such restrictions, in common with discriminatory import licensing, give rise to increased costs through the restriction of choice among buyers and of competition among suppliers. Moreover, there are three distinct additional costs of export-restraint agreements. One is that the importing (protecting) country surrenders the scarcity rents to the exporters — it now buys its imports at a higher cost than necessary, and this is seldom noticed or understood by the public.[41] (This is of course the sweetener that makes the 'voluntary' in the export-restraint agreements not entirely ludicrous as a description of reality.) The second is that export-restraint agreements of this kind promote cartelization abroad, not without damage to the integrity of the importing country's own competition laws. The third is the damage to the international price system. Whereas a global quota only distorts prices inside the protecting country, export restraints distort international prices as well and true scarcity values of different products may not be expressed anywhere.

The direct effect of trade restrictions on prices and (static) resource allocation has received a great deal of attention in the literature. By contrast, the major *indirect* role of protection in impeding adjustment and economic growth, through its umbrella effect on other market rigidities, is only beginning to be recognized. Mancur Olson, of the University of Maryland, shows that the old saying, 'the tariff is the mother of the trust', helps to explain the apparent paradox between, on the one hand, the observed correlation between openness to foreign trade and a country's economic growth performance and, on the other, the calculations of welfare theorists that the costs of protection typically account for no more than one or two per cent of GDP.[42] Without the shelter from foreign competition provided by import restrictions, the ability of domestic labour and enterprise coalitions to generate and hold a position of market power (including, for enterprises, the power to pass on higher costs to the consumer and still make a normal profit) is greatly circumscribed. Protection, therefore, is not just another market impediment on a par with the others, for it plays an important role in sustaining those impediments which depend on the suppression of competition. Liberal trade is the best domestic competition policy that a country can have.[43]

Conventional Fallacies about Trade Liberalization

Vested interests have helped foster three 'conventional wisdoms' about trade liberalization that are either misleading or just plain wrong:

   (a) It must be *multilateral* to be of benefit.
   (b) It will create *unemployment*.
   (c) It should be undertaken *gradually*.

One can begin to expose the fallacies in these popular notions by noting that protection is primarily a device for redistributing income within society. It advances some economic activities by simultaneously retarding or suppressing others. Those activities that require support will normally be the least productive ones, so that in redistributing income to them the aggregate income of the country is reduced.

Kenneth Clements, of the University of Western Australia, and Larry Sjaastad, of the University of Chicago, have shown how, in broad sectoral terms:

(a) the burden of protecting the import-competing sector is largely borne by the export sector, which is unable to pass on the associated increase in material and labour costs and normally receives little assistance itself (this implicit tax results in the relative contraction of the export sector); and

(b) the 'true' protection received by the import-competing sector will always be some fraction of the nominal amount, determined by the extent to which its own costs increase as a result of that protection.[44]

Furthermore, while the protection of the import-competing sector will on average punish the export sector, in no country is that protection uniform among all import-competing industries and firms. Those activities receiving relatively low levels of assistance from the government will in many cases be worse off than they would have been without the protection regime.

To return to the 'conventional wisdoms'. The first one, about the need for *multilateral* reductions in protection, is contradicted by the fact that unilateral trade liberalization will in itself lead to an income-increasing re-allocation of resources, which benefits the liberalizing country irrespective of the trade policy actions of other countries.

As to the second argument, about *unemployment*, it is indeed probable that the initial shift in resources will be from labour-intensive to capital-intensive activities in developed countries, but a large part of the incremental income resulting from an overall rise in productivity will be spent on 'home goods', such as services, which are themselves predominantly labour-intensive. Moreover, those tradeable activities that receive a fillip from trade liberalization will not just be the existing 'traditional' ones, but also new activities which had never had a chance to emerge under the previous regime. As Professors Clements and Sjaastad show, these will tend to be activities with a factor-mix (labour requirement) similar to that of the protected ones.

Finally, the third notion, that a *gradual approach* is superior, assumes that trade liberalization would result in a massive transitional dislocation of the economy. But many 'protected' activities are actually being indirectly taxed under typical protection systems and would thus receive a stimulus from trade liberalization. Even industries which are truly protected will not disappear entirely, for all industries have some activities which are more profitable than others and that are capable of being maintained even in a free trade world.

NOTES AND REFERENCES

1. See Tumlir, 'Government Responsibility for Industrial Restructuring', in Susan Strange and Roger Tooze (eds), *The International Politics of Surplus Capacity* (London: Allen & Unwin, 1981); and Burton, *op. cit.*

2. The seminal article on this is Friedrick A. Hayek, 'The Use of Knowledge in Society', *American Economic Review*, September 1945. An important book in the same tradition is by Thomas Sowell, *Knowledge and Decisions* (New York: Basic Books, 1980).

3. The 'anticipatory' function of the price system is often overlooked by those proposing special government policies for this purpose. See, for example, Lawrence G. Franko, *Industrial Policy in Europe: Solution or Problem?* (Geneva: Centre d'Etudes Industrielles, 1978), quoted in Wolf, *op. cit.*, p. 157.

4. For an extensive empirical investigation of the adverse effects of price distortions on economic growth in developing countries, see Ramgopal Agarwala, *Price Distortions and Growth in Developing Countries*, Staff Working Paper No. 575 (Washington: World Bank, 1983).

5. See, for example: George E. Johnson, 'Do Structural Employment and Training Programs Influence Unemployment', *Challenge*, New York, May-June 1979; James Hughes and Ian Brinkley, 'The Measurement of Secondary Labour Market Effects

Associated with Government Training', *Scottish Journal of Political Economy*, Glasgow, February 1980; *A Medium Term Strategy for Employment and Manpower Policies* (Paris: OECD Secretariat, 1978); *Annual Report 1976-77* (Canberra: Industries Assistance Commission, 1977) and Wolf, *op. cit.*, p. 157.

6. Ironically, the most mobile workers are liable to be those who are relatively highly skilled and well paid, with a financial and psychological incentive to pursue work in their special field. The amount of money needed to 'tip the scales' in a worker's relocation decision is likely to be greatest for the categories of labour which are the lowest paid and the least productive.

7. Studies in the United States have revealed that unemployment rates are significantly higher in those States in which a greater proportion of the labour force is organized. Internationally, the United States has a relatively low degree of unionization and its labour markets have been clearly out-performing those in Western Europe in recent years. See Mancur Olson, *The Rise and Decline of Nations* (New York: Yale University Press, 1982) p. 219, and *The Employment Outlook* (Paris: OECD Secretariat, 1984). In addition, see Brendan M. Walsh, 'Employment and Competitiveness in the European Community, *The World Economy*, March 1984.

8. The unimportance of this practice in the United States helps explain the spontaneous rejuvenation of regions that had been in decline, whereas 'regional problems' have accumulated in Western Europe.

9. Gottfried Haberler, 'Economic Malaise and a Positive Programme for a Benevolent and Enlightened Dictator', in Fritz Machlup, Gerhard Fels and Hubertus Müller-Groeling (eds), *Reflections on a Troubled World Economy: Essays in Honour of Herbert Giersch* (London: Macmillan, for the Trade Policy Research Centre, 1983) p. 217.

10. See George J. Stigler, 'The Economics of Minimum Wage Legislation', *American Economic Review*, June 1946; and, for a survey of the literature, see Charles Brown, Curtis Gilroy and Andrew Cohen, 'The Effect of the Minimum Wage on Employment and Unemployment', *Journal of Economic Literature*, June 1982.

11. Yale Brozen, 'The Effect of Statutory Minimum-wage Increases on Teenage Unemployment', *Journal of Law and Economics*, April 1969; Walter E. Williams, *Youth and Minority Unemployment* (Stanford: Hoover Institution Press, 1978); and John Martin, *Effects of the Minimum Wage on the Youth Labour Market in North America and France* (Paris: OECD Secretariat, 1983).

12. The unemployment rate for the 'under 24s' was estimated at 1.2 per cent in 1984. See 'Swiss Training is Best in West', *Financial Times*, London and Frankfurt, 3 August 1984.

13. Sowell, *op. cit.*, p. 174.

14. See John Gennard, 'Job Security and Industrial Relations', mimeograph, OECD Secretariat, Paris, 1979.

15. A.G.B. Fisher, *Economic Progress and Social Security* (London: Macmillan, 1945) p. 26.

16. David L. Birch, 'Who Creates Jobs', *The Public Interest*, New York, Fall 1981.

17. See Martin Feldstein, 'The Private and Social Cost of Unemployment', *American Economic Review* (Papers and Proceedings), May 1978. Also see Hermione Parker, *The Moral Hazard of Social Benefits* (London: Institute of Economic Affairs, 1983) where it is noted: 'The argument about unemployment should be not about whether today's unemployed genuinely want to work, but about the price at which it is worth their while to sell their labour and the speed with which they look for and find new jobs' (p. 110).

18. Government is a hierarchical or 'vertical' information processing system, whereas the competitive enterprises and individuals in the market process information 'horizontally'. It should be clear that vertical processing will be much less effective than horizontal processing of information. There will be delays and imperfections ('noise') in the flows of information to and from the hierarchical decision maker, not all of which will occur involuntarily or spontaneously. Much of the distortion in the upward flow will result from the efforts of subordinates to filter information so as to make it more presentable to their superiors.

19. On this aspect, see Lawrence Seltzer, 'The Mobility of Capital', *Quarterly Journal of Economics*, Cambridge, Massachussetts, May 1932.

20. See Stigler, 'Imperfections in the Capital Market', *Journal of Political Economy*, June 1967.

21. See, Geoffrey Wood, 'Competition, Innovation, Consumer Protection and the Role of the Market', in Malcolm Fisher (ed.), *A New Financial Revolution* (Sydney: Centre for Independent Studies, 1982). Mr Wood considers three kinds of market failure and concludes that none are of importance in capital markets.

22. *Business Week*, New York, 5 March 1984.

23. *The Economist*, London, 24 September 1983.

24. See Feldstein, *Inflation, Tax Rules and Capital Formation* (Chicago and London: University of Chicago Press, 1983). For a

theoretical treatment of the effects of taxation on risk-taking, see Joseph E. Stiglitz, 'Effect of Wealth, Income and Capital Gains Taxation on Risk Taking', *Quarterly Journal of Economics*, May 1969.

25. Stigler, *loc. cit.*, p. 290.

26. See the revealing record of the parliamentary debate in the United Kingdom on the Restrictive Trade Practices (Stock Exchange) Bill, which was seeking to exempt the stock exchange from the Restrictive Trade Practices Act of 1976 in *British Information Service Survey*, London, December 1983, pp. 434-36.

27. For a general discussion of the real effects of inflation, see Axel Leijonhufvud, *Inflation and Economic Performance* (Tübingen: J.C.B. Mohr, for the Institut für Weltwirtschaft an der Universität Kiel, 1983).

28. *International Trade 1982-83* (Geneva: GATT Secretariat 1983) p. 20.

29. For a concise survey of the literature, see S. Shenoy, 'The Sources of Monopoly', *New Individualist Review*, Chicago, Spring 1966. Also see Joe Bain, 'Conditions of Entry and the Emergence of Monopoly', in E.H. Chamberlin (ed.), *Monopoly and Competition and Their Regulation* (New York: Macmillan Press, 1954).

30. Robert H. Bork, *The Anti-trust Paradox: a Policy at War with Itself* (New York: Basic Books, 1978).

31. Note that even natural monopolies can have their rents bid away. See Demsetz, 'Why Regulate Utilities?', *Journal of Law and Economics*, April 1968.

32. This is illustrated at the international level by the regular crises in the periodic policy meetings of OPEC and also the International Air Transport Association (IATA). For an interesting discussion, see Olson *op. cit.*, p. 58. The sixth 'implication' of his 'logic' of collective action is stated as follows: 'Distributional coalitions make decisions more slowly than the individuals and firms of which they are comprised, tend to have crowded agendas and bargaining tables, and more often fix prices than quantities.'

33. See, for example, the interview with Wolfgang Kartte, President of West Germany's Federal Cartel Office, in the *International Herald Tribune*, Paris, 13 and 14 October 1984.

34. For analyses of regulated cartels in the United States, see Robert Poole (ed.), *Instead of Regulation: Alternatives to Federal Regulatory Agencies* (Lexington: D.C. Heath, 1982). See also Edmund Kitch, Marc Isaacson and Daniel Kasper, 'The Regulation of Taxicabs in Chicago', *Journal of Law and Economics*, October 1971.

35. For details, see *The Role of Competition Policy in a Period of Economic Recession with Special Reference to Crisis Cartels* (Paris: OECD Secretariat, 1981). On the fallacies in crisis cartels, see Tumlir, 'Salvation Through Cartels? On the Revival of a Myth', *The World Economy*, October 1978.

36. *Review of Agricultural Policies in OECD Member Countries* (Paris: OECD Secretariat, 1983).

37. For details, see the annual reports of the International Trade Commission of the United States, entitled *The Operation of the Trade Agreements Program.*

38. Note that quotas are sometimes defended as an adjustment instrument, in that they could be gradually expanded until they no longer constrain the market at all. (The MFA has sometimes been rationalized in this way, on which point see Gray, 'Senile Industry Protection: a Proposal', *loc. cit.*) This ignores their transitional costs and the political difficulty of phasing them out.

39. For a theoretical analysis and appraisal of the experience with such an approach in Australia, see *Annual Report 1982-83* (Canberra: Industries Assistance Commission, 1983).

40. For detailed analyses of export restraints, see Brian Hindley, 'Voluntary Export Restraints and the GATT's Main Escape Clause', *The World Economy*, November 1980; and Kent Jones, 'The Political Economy of Voluntary Restraint Agreements' *Kyklos*, Vol. 37, 1984.

41. The rational reaction of an exporter who is required by an export-restraint agreement to reduce the level of his sales to a particular market is to raise his selling price until demand has fallen to the new, reduced level of supply, thus recouping some of his lost revenue. For a quantitative assessment of the effect of voluntary export-restraint agreements, see David Greenaway and Hindley, *What Britain Pays for Voluntary Export Restraints*, Thames Essay No. 43 (London: Trade Policy Research Centre, 1985).

42. Olson, *op. cit.* See also Richard Blackhurst, Nicolas Marian and Tumlir, *Adjustment, Trade and Growth in Developed and Developing Countries*, *op. cit.*

43. Note the curious omission of protection from the impediments to well-functioning markets described by Assar Lindbeck in 'Industrial Policy as an Issue in the Economic Environment', *The World Economy*, December 1981.

44. Clements and Sjaastad, *op. cit.*

Chapter 6

The Political Problem of Adjustment

'Democracy, if it survives, must above all learn how to discipline and deorganize such minorities as special-interest pressure groups'

— Henry Simons,
Economic Policy for a Free Society (1948)

THERE is heavy irony in the fact that governments, having impaired the information function of the price system through inflation and market-sharing devices sustained by protection, to the point where investment wilts, unemployment grows and (government-financed) 'excess capacity' co-exists with bottlenecks in supply, should then justify an even more active industrial role for themselves on the grounds that markets 'can't cope'.[1] When industry groups, attracted by a promising new source of profits, clamour for public assistance, this is taken by governments as further evidence that they cannot be expected to stand on their own feet.

The main impediments to adjustment and growth identified in the preceding chapter have arisen through government efforts to help various producer groups. Such efforts cannot but make for bad policy. There is no way — scientific, rational or magic — of reconciling the 'needs' of different producers; that is to say, no way for governments. The competing claims of producers on resources can be reconciled only by *consumers*, as Adam Smith recognized so long ago:

'Consumption is the sole end and purpose of all production; and the interest of the producer ought to be attended to only so far as it may be necessary for promoting that of the consumer. The maxim is so perfectly self-evident that it would be absurd to attempt to prove it.'[2]

It is inevitable that policy measures which pay no heed to the consumer will end up harming society at large, irrespective of the transitory gains to special-interest groups.

ECONOMIC POLICY AS INCOME
REDISTRIBUTION

Yet governments nearly always present public assistance to producer groups as legitimate policy promoting the interest of the nation as a whole and the public has become accustomed to the idea.[3] The purely *redistributive* nature of most economic policy is not generally understood. For example, the large literature which now exists on regulation makes it quite clear that most regulatory agencies were either established at the behest, or gradually came under the control, of the interest to be regulated, although being justified on a public-interest rationale. Labour market policy largely consists of measures for fixing wages, or allowing unions to do so, in ways such that income is redistributed away from certain groups within the labour force (youths, those in disadvantaged regions).[4] In the various forms of industrial policy ('rescue' operations, support for promising activities) and agricultural price and income policies, the redistributive intent is virtually unconcealed.

Foreign trade policy, too, is pure redistribution, although here again it is masked by the rhetoric of national interest. For example, since the mid-1970s, Western governments have gone to great lengths to convince their electorates that Japan is up to no good in her trade policies. While most of their accusations have no basis in fact,[5] this tactic has permitted the governments concerned to justify costly discriminatory protection against Japanese goods as 'retaliatory' or 'countervailing' measures, taken in the public interest (although outside the relevant legal procedures established for that purpose).

Even the standard macro-economic policies, as pursued in recent years, have been substantially redistributive, not just in effect but also in intent. It would be very difficult to argue that the Great Inflation of the 1970s was just a purposeless accident, or that the budget deficits — continued government expenditure beyond the limits sanctioned by the electorate — persist for reasons other than inflexible distributive claims or entitlements.[6]

What is most objectionable about such policies, however, is not just their redistributive nature — it can be argued that redistributing income is a legitimate and even necessary function of the democratic political process[7] — but that they are effected through measures which are both surreptitious and extremely costly to society as a whole. Their surreptitious nature consists both in being presented as something else and, more importantly, in the lack of transparency surrounding them. The smaller part of this redistribution, it could be argued, takes place through public budgets; the bulk of it involves measures directed at controlling prices and quantities of goods and services. It is these measures that are the chief impediments to adjustment and growth.

It should be clear, therefore, that the 'problem of adjustment' as presented by governments is a false one. There is no *technical* difficulty for economic policy-makers at all. A rational adjustment policy would proceed in two stages:

first, governments would discontinue the policies that are known to be impeding adjustment;

then they would wait a while, to see whether some additional (active) intervention may be needed.

After all, economic policy is merely experiment; and progress, as in science, depends on learning from failures. The fact that governments have instead persisted in adding further layers of redistributive interventions on top of the old ones confirms that the underlying problem is not technical but political.

POLITICAL MARKET

The 'asymmetries' in the political market-place which favour producer groups over consumers and taxpayers are well known.[8] The key to political influence lies in organization. Organization facilitates communication with political representatives, allows block-voting threats, mobilization of campaign resources (funds, propaganda) *et cetera*. For these reasons, politicians will prefer to deal with organized groups and may even assist in their formation.[9] Nevertheless, there are considerable obstacles to organizing a group for collective action, whether to obtain a benefit (subsidy) from government or to avoid a burden (tax), where that action will eventually benefit *all* the potential members of the group whether they sign up or not. This is the 'free rider' problem.[10] It is most intractable for large, regionally-diffuse groups, such as consumers and taxpayers, and least so for small groups, such as producers, where communication is easier and the expected pay-off to individual members is substantial.

So it is inevitable that governments will be under pressure to make policy changes which redistribute income to producer groups at collective cost. This is a fact of political life. But it does not follow that pressure groups must inevitably get their own way. Whether the democratic political system will succumb to their demands — that is, whether there will be 'political failure' — is crucially dependent on the consequent political discussion.

Frank Knight, the distinguished American economist, outlined the steps necessary for an 'intelligent' (legitimate) political decision-making process.[11] If a policy is to have a reasonable chance of improving a situation, certain steps are necessary:

(a) it must first be decided what is most likely to happen in the natural course of events (that is, in the absence of additional interventions);

(b) then it must be decided what interventions are feasible, given the instruments available to government;

(c) after which, the most likely consequences of each must be assessed;

(d) whereupon, an agreed ranking of the alternatives must be made, reflecting the value judgments of the political representatives; and,

(e) finally, the values themselves (and their weight) must be scrutinized anew for each policy issue under discussion.

It is not difficult to believe that few, if any, government measures impeding adjustment could have withstood such rigorous political scrutiny. In a political forum where all interests are represented, proposals to 'reassign' income to particular groups, at collective cost, should have difficulty attracting majority support. This is because any reassignment of income will have adverse effects on other interest groups, in addition to the effects on the large mass of (unorganized) consumers and taxpayers. (For example, a proposal to restrict basic steel imports would normally be opposed by the motor vehicle, construction and other user industries, each of which would have political representation, being more important in certain electorates than the steel industry.)[12]

Interest groups are a necessary element of democracy. They are the soil from which political ideas sprout. But in the original conception, these ideas were to be refined by discussion between and among groups, with political *agreements* determining the form of their final implementation. Had there been a thorough discussion of the economic 'problem' of adjustment, the ultimate conclusions could not have been very different from those reached here, namely stop doing what is known to be wrong. So what went wrong? What made it possible for governments to act on the ideas and wishes of each group *before* these ideas could be refined and reconciled through a general discussion?

ADMINISTRATIVE DISCRETION

What has happened in many cases is that legislatures have passed laws in sufficiently vague terms that they can be agreed to be in the public interest. It has been left to the administration to take care of the 'details'. This has given the executive enormous discretionary power and led to the implementation of many measures on which political agreement would not have been possible.

The growth of bilateral export-restraint agreements involving the United States illustrates this perfectly. The two standard opening gambits for negotiating a 'voluntary' export restraint in that country are (i) a threat of import quotas or (ii) an allegation of subsidization.

In the first case, when a group of congressmen introduce a bill in the Congress mandating discriminatory quotas, the Administration will open negotiations to obtain an export-restraint agreement with the countries affected on the basis of 'avoiding a greater evil'. But the whole process is an empty bluff. It is doubtful whether such a bill could attract majority support and, even if it did, the executive would be obliged to veto it because of the country's obligations under the GATT.

In the second case, the Administration depends on the desire of the exporting countries to avoid a drawn-out, costly and uncertain subsidy proceeding. But the provision in the Trade Act of 1974, which effectively permits export restraint as an alternative to countervailing duties, is improper delegation because it is essentially uncontrollable and thus subject to abuse.

Both kinds of procedure achieve the following accommodation: through administrative action, small groups of legislators can satisfy narrow constituency interests without having to persuade a legislative majority that that action is in all their interests.

Elsewhere, the extent of administrative discretion in the reassignment of income is perhaps most apparent in the area of 'industrial policy'. For example, the United Kingdom's Industry Act of 1972 empowered the Government to grant subsidies to new ventures which in its opinion were 'viable', but unable to get adequate finance from private sources.[13] The dangers were noted by some at the time.[14] In Canada, the Regional Development Incentives Act authorizes the Department of Regional Economic Expansion to subsidize investment projects where 'it is probable that the facility would

[not] be established ... without the provision of such an incentive'.[15] Numerous other examples could be given.

In essence, the bureaucracy is being left in these cases to judge what is in the public interest. But the 'public interest' can only be evaluated through a political agreement; the bureaucracy is not appropriate for this task. What is more, bureaucracy has interests of its own, which it can best pursue by using its discretionary powers to support *private* interests.

If one begins with the observation that bureaucrats are human beings, it is natural to suppose that their behaviour will be at least partly motivated by self-interest and not, as welfare theory has implicitly assumed, by altruism alone.[16] While the self-interests of the private entrepreneurs are promoted by profit-seeking, however, those of the bureaucrat are necessarily confined to other goals: salary, security, prestige, power (or the illusion of it) *et cetera*. All of these are positively related to an administrative department's size and influence. If, as in many cases, the department was initially created to provide a communication link between government and some part of the community, a symbiotic relationship will naturally develop between that department and its 'client'. As Sir Anthony Rawlinson and Sir Brian Hayes, when joint permanent secretaries of the Department of Trade and Industry in the United Kingdom, expressed it in 1984:

> 'One of the main functions of a department such as ours is to provide a channel of contact and, one hopes, of understanding between government and the business world. This is a two way activity. As we cultivate relations with the business world we hope they will cultivate relations with the government through the department... The first role of our sponsorship divisions is to get to know their industries really well and enable the industry to know whom they should approach whenever they have a problem of any kind that involves government.'[17]

The outcome is that the bureaucracy tends to be captured by the special-interest pressure groups in the private sector. This is not to suggest that the public servants concerned are acting improperly; only that the 'public' whom they are serving is a rather narrow segment of the whole.

This means, first, that when the legislature leaves decisions bearing on income distribution to the administration, the perverse situation arises, in a democracy, whereby law is made in practice by minorities (an opposite 'tyranny' to that of traditional concern). Secondly, when political decision-makers wish to evaluate policy changes being demanded by pressure groups, the advice they receive from the bureaucracy will be biased.

The interest-group conception of bureaucracy also explains why national administrations welcome a state of politics in which every policy mistake becomes an untouchable accomplishment of a particular group, so that a 'correction' must take the ('second-best') form of getting around it by superimposing a new, bureaucracy-expanding, programme (such as adjustment assistance). In this way, a multi-directional, largely self-cancelling, but extremely costly system of transfers has emerged and redistribution appears to have become the main function of the state.[18]

'POLITICAL FAILURE': THE 'CONSTITUTIONAL' APPROACH

The term 'political failure' is sometimes wrongly interpreted as implying a failure of politicians or bureaucrats. This is no more true than market failure could be held to imply a failure of economic agents. In both cases, failure results from the fact that adequate information is not, or cannot be, brought to bear on decisions. In the economic market, this arises either because property rights are not specified (to air or a stream) or where quasi-property rights (free entry into an industry) are not protected. In the political market, it is due to the absence of, or tolerated disregard for, rules and institutions for structuring and informing political decision-making.

This shows the essentially *constitutional* nature of 'political failure', constitutions being rules for the making of rules. Reforms are needed to ensure that collective decisions are made through an adequately informed political discussion. The task is to establish procedural devices which could serve to minimize political failure in the same way that decentralization — competition and private property rights — minimizes market failure.

Revival of the 'Delegation Doctrine'

First, it is clearly important that the discussion should actually take place in a political forum, so that substantive political decisions are not left to the bureaucracy. In a governmental system of separated powers, legislatures should dictate public policy only by majority vote. There is nothing radical about such a proposition. It is the substance of the ancient delegation doctrine in constitutional law, *delegata potestas non potest delegari* (a delegated power cannot be delegated),[19] or in common-law countries the 'law of the agency'.

'The maxim *delegata potestas non potest delegari* is not one of the more technical 'terms of the art' of the law; it is really a matter of plain common sense and common experience. If I ask a friend to exercise a power of attorney on my behalf, I do so because I have confidence in him; and he would frustrate my purpose if, without my authority, he appointed somebody else for me. On the other hand, I should not expect him to attend on every routine detail himself and I could not complain if he employed typists, secretaries, brokers, bankers and the like in the ordinary course of business for common transactions. This is the doctrine as applied to the commercial law of agency — in so far as the principal relies on the personal qualifications of the agent, duties cannot be delegated...'[20]

The function of the doctrine is precisely to ensure that the legislature does not evade its essential responsibility, which is to choose between the policy alternatives pressed upon it by the political process. Thus, in instructing the national administration to deal with a problem, it must provide proper standards for the implementation of policy measures. The ostensible function of these 'standards' is to provide guidance to the courts, but the requirement also ensures that the issue will be discussed thoroughly by the legislature and that the electorate will be educated by that discussion. The discussion which would be required for a proper delegation of legislative power would lead to a more comprehensive understanding of the consequences of pursuing political objectives and of the 'trade-offs' among them.

Although clearly constitutional in character, the reactivation of the delegation doctrine would require no constitutional amendments (nor even a formal constitution). The main prospect for reform is through the courts. Indeed, since the 1970s, cases have been multiplying in American and, to a lesser extent, in West European courts in which private parties complain of arbitrary and unreasonable exercise of the trade-regulatory powers delegated to national executives.[21] As they respond to these complaints, the courts will eventually have to question the mode of the delegation itself.[22]

A 'Transparency Institution'

A second procedural device for raising the quality of information bearing on political decisions has been attracting some attention recently.[23] It involves the establishment of an independent 'transparency institution' whose sole function would be to provide information to policy-makers and the community about the economy-wide implications of government measures which reassign income to special-interest groups. This information is under-supplied at present not only because the political process does not demand it but also because the typically fragmented ('sponsorship') bureaucracies have neither the incentive nor the capability of supplying it.

To inform political discussion adequately, a transparency institution would need the following powers:

(a) to advise governments on the national welfare effects of all proposed public assistance/protection to all productive sectors before any decision can be taken;

(b) to publicize this advice, preferably at the same time that it goes to government; and

(c) to undertake a continuous systematic survey and economic appraisal of the existing stock of public assistance (border protection, subsidies, regulations *et cetera*), the details of which must also be publicized periodically.

The transparency institution should not have any executive or judicial power, its role should be confined to improving the quality and availability of information. To perform this task effectively, it would need to be designed in such a way as to ensure its independence, impartiality and continuity.

In considering whether to establish such a body, governments might have misgivings about possible usurpation of their political role. But to the extent that the transparency institution improved the understanding of government and the electorate about the long-term, economy-wide effects of assistance to industries, it would increase the power of government to serve the national interest, not lessen it. Naturally, vested interests could be expected to resist the establishment of a transparency institution. In this case, however, their lobbying would be so obviously self-seeking and contrary to the public interest that its effectiveness would be undermined.

It should be made clear that the sort of institution proposed differs in vital respects from the 'tariff boards' found in such countries as New Zealand, Canada and the United States. These bodies are mainly occupied with quasi-judicial questions, such as whether an industry has suffered 'injury' from imports, whether foreign competition is 'unfair' *et cetera*; they do not promote transparency in the broad sense. As J.M Finger, of the World Bank, has shown, the charter and procedures of institutions such as the International Trade Commission in the United States are inherently biased in favour of the producers, effectively disenfranchising those (larger) sections of the community who bear the costs of protection.[24] Indeed, their main purpose seems to be to obfuscate and to relieve the legislature from the burden of making decisions, rather than to educate legislators and the community and to crystallize the issues on which decisions must be made. A more appropriate precedent for a transparency institution is the Industries Assistance Commission in Australia.[25]

A Non-discrimination Trade Treaty

Our discussion of the 'impediments' to adjustment and growth revealed the key role of border protection. Without protection against imports, neither cartels (in product and labour markets) nor subsidies would pose such a problem. (If steel could be imported into the European Community without quantitative limitations, subsidy needs would soon exceed the capacity of national budgets.)

Protection at the present levels is possible mainly because it can be discriminatory. In those periods in the past in which the most-favoured-nation (MFN) commitment was by and large observed, levels of protection were stable or declining. The MFN principle mobilizes the latent mercantilism, especially of the large countries, into a mutually countervailing pattern. A country wanting to raise the protection it was granting to an industry had to negotiate with others, offer a compensating reduction in another import barrier, or suffer their retaliation. In this way, the principle also mobilizes the power of the large countries on behalf of the main interest of the small countries, which is that they should be treated equally. Non-discriminatory protection is also relatively transparent, that is to say, its costs are more clearly visible. For these reasons, legislative insistence that national trade policy should be conducted on the basis of non-discrimination has, through historic precedent, provided the necessary guiding standard for, and a constraint on, the delegated discretionary powers needed by national executives for the conduct of commercial diplomacy.

The reinstatement of the MFN principle would represent a simple procedure for freezing and ultimately reducing the levels of protection. It would be sufficient if only a limited number of core countries, bearing the main (and, for practical purposes, all) responsibility for the international economic order, accepted the commitment. All members of the GATT are bound by it already; the trouble is that, like European Community law, the principle has been disregarded in the conduct of actual policy. This is able to happen because the GATT is not a real treaty which binds national legislatures and legislatures have therefore delegated to their national administrations powers in trade policy which allow discrimination. If the MFN principle could be entrenched against legislative delegation, the whole GATT system would be strengthened as its own non-discrimination provisions became effectively enforceable.

There are only two ways of accomplishing such an entrenchment. One is by constitutional amendment. But this is clearly out of the question. The other is by *treaty*. It is hard to find an important reason which would make it infeasible for, say, the seven governments which gather annually at the Economic Summit meetings to conclude a treaty among themselves stipulating that, as of a certain date, they will conduct their policy strictly on the basis of unconditional MFN treatment of their trading partners. No great statesmanship is needed. Any politician of average ability should be able to make it clear to his people that in the principle of non-discrimination, national interest and international responsibility perfectly coincide. Or, if this may seem too exacting a view of what to expect from our statesmen and politicians, let us put it another way. If the governments of the major Western countries cannot agree on the desirability of non-discrimination in international economic relations, there is not much on which they could reasonably hope to agree.

NOTES AND REFERENCES

1. See the article by Tumlir and Wolf, 'The Way Back to Sustained Economic Growth', *The World Economy*, June 1983, which

describes how 'there has been a vicious circle from political commitments to inflation and micro-economic distortions and back to still further commitments' (p. 105).

2. Adam Smith, *op. cit.*, p. 660

3. This is far removed from John Stuart Mill's conception of democracy as a continuing course of adult education in the facts of political life.

4. For example, minimum wages are demanded by labour unions and justified by governments as a means of preventing the exploitation of workers, especially youths. But minimum-wage requirements in practice prevent low-skilled and less-experienced job-seekers (youths) from being offered employment, thus preserving the high wages of those already in employment. 'Acceptable' unemployment benefits are then demanded by unions to make this inequitable situation more tolerable to the losers. On the 'special interest' rationale for various labour-market policies, see Dan C. Heldman, James T. Bennett and Manuel H. Johnson, *Deregulating Labor Relations* (Dallas, Texas: Fisher Institute, 1981).

5. See Gary R. Saxonhouse, 'What's All This about "Industrial Targeting" in Japan?', *The World Economy*, September 1983, and 'The Micro- and Macro-economics of Foreign Sales to Japan', in William R. Cline (ed.), *Trade Policy in the 1980s* (Washington: Institute for International Economics, 1983); Philip H. Tresize, 'Industrial Policy is Not the Major Reason for Japan's Success', *The Brookings Review*, Washington, Spring 1983; Radha Sinha, 'Japan's Concessions Towards Trade Fairness: Mistaken Western Views', *Intereconomics*, Hamburg, September-October 1982; Gary Banks, 'The Japanese Trade Threat: Myths and Realities', mimeograph, Trade Policy Research Centre, London, 1982; James Y. Bourlet, *Opinion, Economics and the EEC: Half Truths for Britain and Japan* (London: Open Seas Forum, 1984); and *Report of the Japan-United States Economic Relations Group*, Prepared for the President of the United States and the Prime Minister of Japan (Washington: Japan-United States Economic Relations Group, 1981).

6. Professor Kindleberger has put it this way: 'When all groups demand 110 per cent of the national income, and government is unable to resist them, 10 per cent inflation is inevitable.' Kindleberger, 'The Aging Economy', *Weltwirtschaftliches Archiv*, Kiel, No. 3, Vol. 114, 1978, p. 419.

7. Dan Usher, *The Economic Prerequisite to Democracy* (New York: Columbia University Press, 1981 and Oxford: Basil Blackwell, 1981).

8. The seminal analyses are Anthony Downs, *An Economic Theory of Democracy* (New York: Harper & Row, 1957), and Olson, *The Logic of Collective Action* (New Haven: Yale University Press, 1965).

9. Peter Aranson, 'Can Democratic Societies Reform Themselves?', in *For a Free Society in the Coming Decade* (Berlin: Mount Pelerin Society, 1982).

10. Olson, *The Logic of Collective Action, op. cit.*

11. Frank Knight, *Intelligence and Democratic Action* (Cambridge, Massachusetts: Harvard University Press, 1960).

12. Such opposition has been weakened in the past by the expectation that compensatory protection could be obtained.

13. See 'Government Support for Industry: Guide to Schemes of Selective Financial Assistance', *Trade and Industry*, London, 19 January 1979.

14. See Denton and O'Cleireacain, *Subsidy Issues in International Commerce*, Thames Essay No. 5 (London: Trade Policy Research Centre, 1972), especially the Preface where the authors wrote:

'What is alarming about the Industry Act 1972 is the absence from its provisions of any meaningful criteria for granting assistance [to particular industries]. Nor are there laid down any conditions under which government assistance should be granted. It is not enough to depend on the usual checks and balances of the Whitehall system of government to ensure that public resources are not squandered on economically unsound or inefficiently managed enterprises. Notwithstanding the White Paper and a number of ministerial statements on the subject, little effort can seriously be said to have been made yet to develop a coherent policy for assisting regions, firms and workers to adjust to changing economic circumstances.

'The absence of publicly known and clearly enunciated criteria and conditions for government assistance amounts to an open invitation to firms in competitive difficulty to resort to political pressure for subsidy support or special protection. Any outside advice on government intervention in industry (and trade) should be representative of the public interest in the broadest sense, including consumer interests and the interests of competitively strong industries, besides independent economic opinion. It is ironic, and even disturbing, that while the Industry Act was passing through Parliament both the Expenditure Committee and the Public Accounts Committee in the House of Commons were actually preparing and publishing reports that expressed grave disquiet over the way in which interventions in industry under previous governments have been managed.'

In this last connection, see *Public Money in the Private Sector*, Sixth Report of the Expenditure Committee (London: Her Majesty's Stationery Office, 1972); and *Third Report of the Committee of Public Accounts: Session 1971-72* (London: Her Majesty's Stationery Office, 1972).

15. Usher, *op. cit.*, p. 134.

16. 'Government may not have acted, in Meade-Tinbergen fashion, in the general interest — all wise and all just.' See Kindleberger, *Government and International Trade, op. cit.*, p. 8.

17. 'Using a Voice in Whitehall', *British Business*, London, 21 September 1984, p. 86.

18. See Tullock, *Economics of Income Redistribution* (Amsterdam: Kluwer-Nijhoff, 1983).

19. See Aranson, *op. cit.*, and the quotation from John Locke therein (p. 26).

20. Sir Carleton Allen, *Law and Orders*, second edition (London: Stephens & Sons, 1956) p. 208.

21. For example, in the United States, the Administration's 'country-of-origin' rules for textile and clothing imports were challenged by American importers and retailers at the Court of International Trade in New York on 30 August 1984: 'The suit accuses the Reagan Administration of violating the Multi-fibre Arrangement... The suit also charges that, domestically, the new rules "violate required administrative procedures" and are "arbitrary, capricious, an abuse of discretion and otherwise contrary to law".' See *Far Eastern Economic Review*, Hong Kong, 13 September 1984, p. 73.

22. The United States Supreme Court, in its June 1983 decision on *US Immigration and Naturalization Service v. Chadha*, has gone a long way to providing a basis for such questioning. The decision, striking down the device of legislative veto, implicitly though effectively reasserts the proper delegation doctrine in the United States. Legislative veto was actually exercised only seldom. Its main function appears to have been to disarm legislative opposition to bills delegating broad discretionary powers. The impact of the decision on the conduct of trade policy, and the international trade regime, can be suggested by a single example. The recent proliferation of protectionist measures discussed earlier reflects, or is rationalized

by, governments' attempts to implement an 'industrial policy', however defined. In many industrial countries, considerable effort has been devoted to securing a legislative basis for such a policy. In the United States that effort has been squashed by the *Chadha* decision. It is inconceivable that a Congressional majority could be assembled for the necessary empowering and appropriation acts devoid of legislative veto provisions.

23. In this connection, see *Transparency for Positive Adjustment* (Paris: OECD Secretariat, 1982); Patrick Messerlin, 'The Political Economy of Protection: the Bureaucratic Case', *Weltwirtschaftliches Archiv*, No. 3, Vol. 117, 1981; and Hugh Corbet, 'Public Scrutiny of Protection: Trade Policy and the Investigative Branch of Government', in *International Trade and the Consumer* (Paris: OECD Secretariat, 1986).

This section also draws on Banks, 'Vested Interests, Domestic Transparency and International Trade Policy', *Intereconomics*, May-June 1984.

24. J.M. Finger, 'Incorporating the Gains from Trade into Policy', *The World Economy*, December 1982. See also Finger, Keith H. Hall and Douglas R. Nelson, 'The Political Economy of Administered Protection', *American Economic Review*, June 1982.

25. On the performance of the Industries Assistance Commission, see *Transparency for Positive Adjustment*, *op. cit.*, and Corbet, 'Public Scrutiny of the Costs and Benefits of Public Assistance to Industries', *Australian Outlook*, Canberra, April 1985.

List of References

THIS list contains only the more important references cited in the text. The reader should refer to the Notes and References at the end of each chapter for more complete bibliographical information.

C. Michael Aho and Thomas A. Bayard, 'American Trade Adjustment Assistance after Five Years', *The World Economy*, November 1980.

Armen A. Alchian, 'Information Costs, Pricing and Resource Unemployment', *Western Economic Journal*, Los Angeles, June 1969.

Gary Banks, 'Vested Interests, Domestic Transparency and International Trade Policy', *Intereconomics*, May-June 1984.

Jagdish N. Bhagwati (ed.), *Import Competition and Response* (Chicago and London: University of Chicago Press, for the National Bureau of Economic Research, 1982).

David L. Birch, 'Who Creates Jobs', *The Public Interest*, New York, Fall 1981.

Richard Blackhurst, Nicolas Marian and Jan Tumlir, *Adjustment, Trade and Growth in Developed and Developing Countries*, GATT Studies in International Trade No. 6 (Geneva: GATT Secretariat, 1978).

James H. Buchanan, Robert D. Tollison and Gordon Tullock (eds), *Toward a Theory of the Rent-Seeking Society* (College Station: Texas A and M University Press, 1980).

John Burton, *Picking Losers? The Political Economy of Industrial Policy*, Hobart Paper No. 99 (London: Institute of Economic Affairs, 1983).

Stephen N.S. Cheung, *The Myth of Social Cost*, Hobart Paper No. 82 (London: Institute of Economic Affairs, 1978).

Kenneth W. Clements and Larry A. Sjaastad, *How Protection Taxes Exporters*, Thames Essay No. 39 (London: Trade Policy Research Centre, 1984).

Hugh Corbet, 'Public Scrutiny of Protection: Trade Policy and the Investigative Branch of Government', in *International Trade and the Consumer* (Paris: OECD Secretariat, 1986).

W.M. Corden, *Trade Policy and Economic Welfare* (Oxford: Clarendon Press, 1974).

Gerard and Victoria Curzon, *Global Assault on Non-tariff Trade Barriers*, Thames Essay No. 3 (London: Trade Policy Research Centre, 1972).

Victoria Curzon Price, *Industrial Policies in the European Community* (London: Macmillan, for the Trade Policy Research Centre, 1981).

Harold Demsetz, 'Information and Efficiency: another Viewpoint', *Journal of Law and Economics*, April 1969.

Geoffrey Denton, Seamus O'Cleireacain and Sally Ash, *Trade Effects of Public Subsidies to Private Enterprises* (London: Macmillan, for the Trade Policy Research Centre, 1975).

James A. Dorn, 'Trade Adjustment Assistance: Case of Goverment Failure', *Cato Journal*, Washington, Winter 1982.

Anthony Downs, *An Economic Theory of Democracy* (New York: Harper and Row, 1957).

MARTIN FELDSTEIN, 'The Private and Social Cost of Unemployment', *American Economic Review* (Papers and Proceedings), May 1978.

MARTIN FELDSTEIN, *Inflation, Tax Rules and Capital Formation* (Chicago and London: University of Chicago Press, 1983).

J.M. FINGER, 'Incorporating the Gains from Trade into Policy', *The World Economy*, London, December 1982.

A.G.B. FISHER, *Economic Progress and Social Security* (London: Macmillan, 1945).

CHARLES FRANK, *Foreign Trade and Domestic Aid* (Washington: Brookings Institution, 1977).

GOTTFRIED HABERLER, 'Economic Malaise and a Positive Programme for a Benevolent and Enlightened Dictator', in Fritz Machlup, Gerhard Fels and Hubertus Müller-Groeling (eds), *Reflections on a Troubled World: Essays in Honour of Herbert Giersch* (London: Macmillan, for the Trade Policy Research Centre, 1983).

FRIEDRICK A. HAYEK, 'The Use of Knowledge in Society', *American Economic Review*, Menasha, Wisconsin, September 1945.

DAN C. HELDMAN, JAMES T. BENNETT and MANUEL H. JOHNSON, *Deregulating Labor Relations* (Dallas, Texas: Fisher Institute, 1981).

BRIAN HINDLEY, 'Voluntary Export Restraints and the GATT's Main Escape Clause', *The World Economy*, London, November 1980.

HAROLD M. HOCHMAN, 'Rule Change and Transitional Equity', in Hochman and G.E. Peterson (eds), *Redistribution Through Public Choice* (New York: Columbia University Press, 1974).

CHARLES KINDLEBERGER, *Government and International Trade*, Princeton Essays in International Finance No. 129 (Princeton: Princeton University, 1978).

CHARLES KINDLEBERGER, 'The Aging Economy', *Weltwirtschaftliches Archiv*, Kiel, No. 3, Vol. 114, 1978.

FRANK KNIGHT, *Intelligence and Democratic Action* (Cambridge, Massachusetts: Harvard University Press, 1960).

ANNE KRUEGER, 'The Political Economy of the Rent-seeking Society', *American Economic Review*, Menasha, Wisconsin, June 1984.

AXEL LEIJONHUFVUD, *Inflation and Economic Performance* (Tübingen: J.C.B. Mohr, for the Institut für Weltwirtschaft an der Universität Kiel, 1983).

ASSAR LINDBECK, 'Industrial Policy as an Issue in the Economic Environment', *The World Economy*, London, December 1981.

PETER J. LLOYD, 'A Knightian Model for the Analysis of Structural Adjustments by Firms', *Weltwirtschaftliches Archiv*, Kiel, No. 4, Vol. 117, 1981.

FRITZ MACHLUP, GERHARD FELS and HUBERTUS MÜLLER-GROELING (eds), *Reflections on a Troubled World Economy: Essays in Honour of Herbert Giersch* (London: Macmillan, for the Trade Policy Research Centre, 1983).

STEPHEN P. MAGEE, 'The Welfare Effects of Restrictions on US Trade', *Brookings Papers on Economic Activity*, Washington, No. 3, 1972.

MICHAEL McKEE and EDWIN G. WEST, 'The Theory of the Second Best: a Solution in Search of a Problem', *Economic Inquiry*, Los Angeles, July 1981.

PATRICK MESSERLIN, 'The Political Economy of Protection: the Bureaucratic Case', *Weltwirtschaftliches Archiv*, Kiel, No. 117, 1981.

96 *List of References*

MANCUR OLSON, *The Rise and Decline of Nations* (New York: Yale University Press, 1982).

MANCUR OLSON, *The Logic of Collective Action* (New Haven: Yale University Press, 1965).

HERMIONE PARKER, *The Moral Hazard of Social Benefits* (London: Institute of Economic Affairs, 1983).

CLARENCE PHILBROOK, 'Realism in Policy Espousal', *American Economic Review*, December, 1953.

ARTHUR C. PIGOU, *The Economics of Welfare* (London: Macmillan 1920).

ROBERT POOLE (ed.), *Instead of Regulation: Alternatives to Federal Regulatory Agencies* (Lexington: D.C. Heath, 1982).

ALAN POWELL and PETER DIXON, *Structural Adaptation in an Ailing Macroeconomy* (Melbourne: Melbourne University Press, 1979).

ADAM SMITH, *An Inquiry into the Nature and Causes of the Wealth of Nations* (Indianapolis: Liberty Press, 1981).

THOMAS SOWELL, *Knowledge and Decisions* (New York: Basic Books, 1980).

GEORGE J. STIGLER, 'The Economics of Minimum Wage Legislation', *American Economic Review*, Menasha, Wisconsin, June 1946.

GEORGE J. STIGLER, 'Imperfections in the Capital Market', *Journal of Political Economy*, June 1967.

GORDON TULLOCK, *Economics of Income Distribution* (Amsterdam: Kluwer-Nijhoff, 1983).

JAN TUMLIR, 'Salvation Through Cartels? On the Revival of a Myth', *The World Economy*, London, October 1978.

JAN TUMLIR, 'Government Responsibility for Industrial Restructuring', in Susan Strange and Robert Tooze (eds),

The International Politics of Surplus Capacity (London: Allen & Unwin, 1981).

JAN TUMLIR and MARTIN WOLF, 'The Way Back to Sustained Economic Growth', *The World Economy*, London, June 1983.

DAN USHER, *The Economic Prerequisite to Democracy* (New York: Columbia University Press, 1981 and Oxford: Basil Blackwell, 1981).

PETER G. WARR, 'The Case Against Tariff Compensation', *The Australian Journal of Agricultural Economics*, August 1978.

MARTIN WOLF, *Adjustment Policies and Problems in Developed Countries*, Staff Working Paper No. 349 (Washington: World Bank, 1979).

Unsigned Official Publications

Adjustment Assistance Measures, TD/121 (Geneva: UNCTAD Secretariat, 1971).

Adjustment for Trade: Studies on Industrial Adjustment Problems and Policies (Paris: OECD Secretariat, 1975).

A Medium Term Strategy for Employment and Manpower Policies (Paris: OECD Secretariat, 1978).

Employment, Trade and North-South Cooperation (Geneva: International Labour Office, 1981).

Positive Adjustment Policies: Managing Structural Change (Paris: OECD Secretariat, 1983).

Transparency for Positive Adjustment (Paris: OECD Publications, 1982).

List of Thames Essays

OCCASIONAL papers of the Trade Policy Research Centre are published under the omnibus heading of Thames Essays. Set out below are the particulars of those published to date.

1 GERARD and VICTORIA CURZON, *Hidden Barriers to International Trade* (1970), 75 pp.

2 T.E. JOSLING, *Agriculture and Britain's Trade Policy Dilemma* (1970), 52 pp.

3 GERARD and VICTORIA CURZON, *Global Assault on Non-tariff Trade Barriers* (1972), 44 pp.

4 BRIAN HINDLEY, *Britain's Position on Non-tariff Protection* (1972), 60 pp.

5 GEOFFREY DENTON and SEAMUS O'CLEIREACAIN, *Subsidy Issues in International Commerce* (1972), 75 pp.

6 GEORGE F. RAY, *Western Europe and the Energy Crisis* (1975), 68 pp.

7 THEODORE GEIGER, JOHN VOLPE and ERNEST H. PREEG, *North American Integration and Economic Blocs* (1975), 65 pp.

8 HUGH CORBET, W.M. CORDEN, BRIAN HINDLEY, ROY BATCHELOR and PATRICK MINFORD, *On How to Cope with Britain's Trade Position* (1977), 80 pp.